THE ASCENT OF THE MIND TO GOD

ROBERTVS BELLARMINVS POLITIAN.°
S.R.E. CARD. TIT. S. MARIÆ IN VIA,
Archiep. Capuanus, Eccl. Catholicæ Rom.
Athleta f or tiſsimus

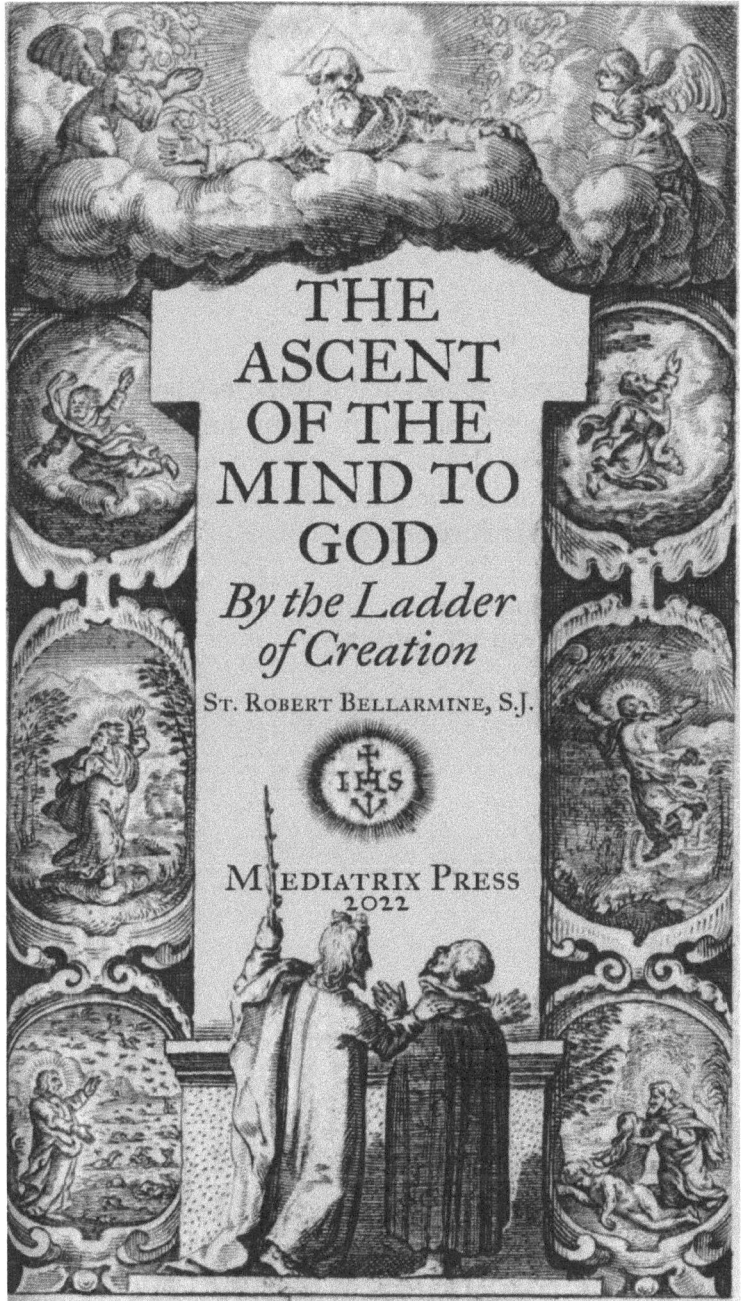

THE ASCENT OF THE MIND TO GOD

By the Ladder of Creation

St. Robert Bellarmine, S.J.

Mediatrix Press
2022

The Ascent of the Mind to God: By the Ladder of Creation

Translated from *De Ascensione Mentis in Deum, per Scalas Rerum Creatarum*, Cologne, 1626.

ISBN: 9781957066097

© Ryan Grant.
All Rights reserved. No part of this work may be reproduced in electronic or physical format, except for quotations for review in journals, blogs, or classroom use without the express permission of the publisher. No part of this work may be placed on archive.org.

Cover art: *The Door Opened* (detail)
British Library Royal 15D II f 117v

Mediatrix Press
607 E 6th St.
Post Falls, ID 83854
www.mediatrixpress.com

Table of Contents

Author's Preface xv

THE FIRST STEP
From the Consideration of Man

Chapter I
The common causes of this consideration 1
Chapter II
God our creator 2
Chapter III
God has created man out of nothing 5
Chapter IV
Man was created in the image of God 7
Chapter V
The beatific vision of God is the intrinsic end of man 11
Chapter VI
The Glory of god and his own eternal salvation is the extrinsic end of man 13

THE SECOND STEP
From the Consideration of the Greater World

Chapter I
The greatness of the world and the greatness of God 17
Chapter II
The multitude of things created and the infinity of the perfection of the creator 19
Chapter III
The variety of created things and God as the infinite source of all good 21
Chapter IV
The inherent virtue in created things, and the omnipotence of God 24

Chapter V
> *The created beauty of things, and the uncreated beauty of God* 27

THE THIRD STEP
From the Consideration of the Earth

Chapter I
> *As our body finds rest upon the earth, so in God alone will our mind find repose.* 31

Chapter II
> *We have our sure foundation upon God* 35

Chapter III
> *The earth nourishes the body by the power of God, who alone nourishes all mankind* 37

Chapter IV
> *The treasures of the earth are, as it were, a shadowing of the eternal good things of God.* . 39

THE FOURTH STEP
From the Consideration of the Waters and Especially of Founts

Chapter I
> *Water washes the stains of the body; God washes the stains of the soul* 43

Chapter II
> *Water extinguishes fire; God quenches the flames of lust* 45

Chapter III
> *Water quenches thirst; God quenches the desires of the heart.* 46

Chapter IV
> *Water joins corporeal things together; God achieves the union of spiritual things* 47

Chapter V
> *Water descends and ascends again; the fount of God's grace gushes forth unto eternal life* 48

Chapter VI
> *A fount of water is the image of God as the fount of our being* 50

Chapter VII
> *God dwelling in himself is the fount of life.* 53

Chapter VIII
> *God the fount of wisdom* 56

THE FIFTH STEP
From the Consideration of the Air

Chapter I
> *The body lives by air, the soul by prayer* 59

Chapter II
> *The air considered as the medium of living, hearing, and speaking.* 62

Chapter III
> *We observe in the air, as it were, a type of the sweetness and mercy of God* 64

Chapter IV
> *Exhortation of the soul to the imitation of the kindness of God* 68

THE SIXTH STEP
From a Consideration of Fire

Chapter I
> *The hatred of God against sin is as a consuming fire* 71

Chapter II
> *Fire perfects the nobler metals, and God crowns the good works of man.* 74

Chapter III
> *Just as fire makes dark iron bright; God leads a sinful soul to knowledge of the truth.* 77

Chapter IV
> *A burning fire welds cold iron; the grace of God restores strength to men's words and deeds.* 80

Chapter V
> *Fire makes hard iron soft; the grace of God conquers the hardness of the heart* 83

Chapter VI
> *Fire thins heavy things; the grace of God directs souls in the way of justice.* 85

THE SEVENTH STEP
From the Consideration of the Heaven, namely the Sun, Moon and Stars

Chapter I
> *The sun, as the tabernacle of the most high and exceedingly beautiful God* 89

Chapter II
> *From the course of the sun the greatness of God appears.* 92

Chapter III
> *The sun gives light and heat; god also gives wisdom and charity* 93

Chapter IV
> *As the moon receives its light from the sun, so the soul truly joined to God, receives pure light* ... 96

Chapter V
> *The moon illuminating the night and leaving us for a time in darkness is a figure of divine grace.* . 99

Chapter VI
> *The arrangement and harmony of the stars presents an image of the heavenly hierarchy* . 101

THE EIGHTH STEP
From the Consideration of the Rational Soul

Chapter I
> *The soul is the created spirit; God is the uncreated spirit and creator of all things* 105

Chapter II
> *The soul is immortal; god eternal* 106

Chapter III
> *The soul is endowed with reason; God is light and understanding* 107

CHAPTER IV
> *The soul has practical knowledge of law; the highest law is in the mind of God* 109

Chapter V
> *The soul of man discovers science; God is the fount of knowledge and wisdom, who invents all things* 110

Chapter VI
> *Man's free will compared with the freedom of God* 111

Chapter VII
> *The rational will of the soul has power to desire spiritual goods; God is himself the highest good, which is charity* 113

Chapter VIII
> *The presence of the soul in the body is a mirror of the existence of God in created things* 114

Chapter IX
> *The soul is in some sense an image of the Most Holy Trinity* 116

Chapter X
> *The soul bestows natural things on the body; God bestows heavenly gifts upon the soul* 117

THE NINTH STEP
> *From The Consideration of the Angels*

Chapter I
> *An angel is altogether a perfect spirit and a created one; God, however, is uncreated and absolutely perfect* 119

Chapter II
> *Of the understanding and knowledge of angels* 120

Chapter III
> *The dominion of the angels over bodies; and the almighty creator* 122

Chapter IV
> *The place and motion of angels, and the omnipresence of God* 124

Chapter V
> *What sort of grace is given to angels, and what to men.* 126

THE TENTH STEP
From the Consideration of God's Essence, by the Similarity of a Corporeal Mass

Chapter I
> *A general consideration of the greatness of God from the four dimensions of corporeal things.* 135

Chapter II
> *The broadness of the essence of God is his immeasurable goodness* 137

Chapter III
> *The breadth of the essence of God is his immeasurable goodness* 139

Chapter IV
> *The length of the divine essence is his eternity* 141

Chapter V
> *The height of God shows the nobility of the divine nature, which is the first effective and most high cause and the final example of all things* 143

Chapter VI
> *God has a lofty throne, for he is the highest king and judge, bringing grace to the humble* 144

Chapter VII
> *the throne of the most high God signifies most blessed rest* 147

Chapter VIII
    Of the manifold depth of the essence of God . . 149

THE ELEVENTH STEP
From the Consideration of the Magnitude of God's Power, by the Similitude of a Corporeal Quantity

Chapter I
    Of the breadth of the power of God. 153
Chapter II
    Of the length of the power of God 155
Chapter III
    Of the height of the power of God 156
Chapter IV
    Of the depth of the power of God 158
Chapter V
    The soul is stirred up to the fear of God and the observance of his commandments 162

THE TWELFTH STEP
From a Consideration of the Magnitude of God's Wisdom through the Similarity of corporeal Magnitude

CHAPTER I
    The breadth of the wisdom of God lies in the perfect knowledge of all things 167
Chapter II
    The length of God's wisdom manifests itself by the knowledge of things to come 169
CHAPTER III
    The height of divine wisdom 171
CHAPTER IV
    The depth of the wisdom of God principally lies in the knowledge of our thoughts which are to come 173
CHAPTER V
    The elevation of the mind to the divine physician, who searches out and cures hearts 175

THE THIRTEENTH STEP
From the Consideration of God's Practical Wisdom

Chapter I
The breadth of his practical wisdom shines forth by reason of the creation of things............ 177

Chapter II
The length of the practical wisdom of God shines forth in the preservation of things 180

Chapter III
The height of God's practical wisdom is seen in the work of our redemption................. 186

CHAPTER IV
The depth of the practical wisdom of God consists in his providence and predestination 191

CHAPTER V
On the depth of the mystery of predestination and reprobation.......................... 195

THE FOURTEENTH STEP
From the Consideration of God's Mercy

Chapter I
The breadth of God's mercy, whereby he removes our miseries 199

Chapter II
The length of the mercy of God is his longanimity or patience 202

Chapter III
The height of the mercy of God is known from the cause moving it 206

Chapter IV
The depth of God's mercy is seen in its effects 208

THE FIFTEENTH STEP
From the Consideration of the Greatness of God's Justice, by the Similitude of a Corporal Quantity

Chapter I
The breadth of God's justice is universal justice 213

Chapter II
The length of God's justice is discovered by its truth and fidelity. 216

Chapter III
The height of God's justice is seen in the bestowal of the heavenly reward. 217

Chapter IV
Of the depth of God's justice, whereby he prepared everlasting punishment for sinners 222

Chapter V
Why the punishment of the damned will be everlasting 227

Author's Preface

THE Holy Scripture admonishes us to seek God with all care.[1] For, "although he be not far from every one of us, since in him we live, and move, and are,"[2] as the Apostle says, yet we are far from God, to the extent that, unless we were continually to dispose our ascent in heart, and ladders that we might raise ourselves to heaven, and seek God with great labor, then we will feed the pigs "in a far off region,"[3] far from our country and Father with the prodigal son.

Now, that we might briefly declare how these things are consistent, that God is not far from us, and nevertheless we are very far off from him, we say: God is not far away from us because he continually sees us, before whose eyes all things are present; likewise he continually thinks of us because "He has care of us,"[4] and he continually touches us because "He carries all things by the word of his power."[5] We, however, are very far from God because we do not see God, nor can we, since he "dwells in an inaccessible light,"[6] while "we are not sufficient of ourselves to think anything about God,"[7] much less can we touch him and cleave to him with pious affection, unless his right hand receive and draw us to him. So, when David said: "My soul hath stuck close to you: your right hand hath received me," he added right after it: "Your right hand has received me."[8] We are not only far

---

[1] Deut. 4:29.

[2] Acts 17:28.

[3] Luke 15:15.

[4] 1 Peter 5:7.

[5] Hebrews 1:3.

[6] 1 Timothy 6:6.

[7] 2 Cor. 3:5.

[8] Psalm 62 (63):9.

from God because we cannot see him, nor easily think of him, nor with affection cleave unto him; but also because being busy with temporal goods, which surround and overwhelm us on every side, we very easily forget God, and with a dry heart our tongue hardly sounds his name in Psalms and sacred prayers.

Consequently, this is the reason why the Holy Spirit, as we were just saying, frequently admonishes us to seek God: "Seek God and your soul shall live;"[9] "Seek his face evermore;"[10] "the Lord is good to them that hope in him, to the soul that seeks him;"[11] "Seek ye the Lord while he may be found;"[12] and "seek him in simplicity of heart;"[13] "When you shall seek there the Lord your God, you shall find him, yet so, if you seek him with all your heart."[14]

Again, this care in searching for God, although it should be common to all the faithful, nevertheless, it pertains more properly to Prelates of the Church, as Sts. Augustine, Gregory, Bernard and other holy fathers witness. Accordingly, they clearly write that a prelate cannot benefit either himself or others unless he were to diligently apply himself in the meditation of divine matters and the refreshment of his own mind. In the City of God, St. Augustine says: "The love of truth seeks holy rest; the necessity of Charity undertakes just business; but neither is the delight of truth to be altogether forsaken, lest, when its sweetness has been withdrawn, the necessity of business will oppress us."[15] Likewise, St. Augustine, when speaking

---

[9] Ps. 68 (69):33.

[10] Ps. 104 (105):4.

[11] Lamentations 3:25.

[12] Isaiah 55:6.

[13] Wisdom 1:1.

[14] Deuteronomy 4:29.

[15] *City of God*, 19, 19.

about himself in *Confessions*, and his frequent meditation on God from creatures: "I often do this: it delights me when I can be spared from my necessary business so as to have recourse unto this pleasure."[16] St. Gregory the Great says, in his book on *Pastoral Care*, "Let a prelate be equal to any in compassion, and before all in contemplation, so that through the depths of piety he might transfer the weakness of others to himself, and by the height of contemplation in seeking after invisible things, he might exceed himself."[17] In the same place, St. Gregory adds the example of Moses and Christ. Moses frequently entered the Tabernacle to contemplate God's secrets, and came out that he might bear with the weakness of his neighbors. Christ himself, by preaching and working miracles during the day, sought the salvation of his neighbors, but he passed the night without sleep in prayer and contemplation. "He passed the whole night in the prayer of God."[18] Many similar things may be read at the end of that chapter.

Moreover, St. Bernard, so as to admonish Pope Eugene (who was at one time his student), not to give himself completely to action but also to recollect himself daily as well as to enjoy holy rest and heavenly food, wrote five books of *Consideration*, in which he not only exhorts him to daily meditation of divine matters, but also to plainly teach him the manner and method of meditation, and thereby to ascend, and by ascending to transform himself into God by understanding and affection. Bernard did not admit that excuse with which we nowadays pretend, namely that he could not make the time for meditation of divine matters due to the business pertaining to the episcopal office. Truly, no one should give himself so much to outward business

---

[16] *Confessions*, 10, 40.

[17] *Reg. Pastor.*, 2, 5.

[18] Luke 6:12.

that he would not leave himself some time to refresh his body with food and drink, or to take sleep. Furthermore, if the body justly seeks this refreshment and rest, how much more does the soul with the utmost justice require food and rest? It cannot truly carry out its duty by any means without this refreshment amid the mass of the greatest affairs. But the food of the soul is prayer and its rest is contemplation, whereby the ascent is prepared in the heart, that "the God of Gods shall be seen in Sion,"[19] as much as he can be seen in this valley of tears.

Still, no other ladder unto God is presented to us mortal men except for the work of God. Those who, by the singular gift of God have been admitted into Paradise by another way, so as to hear the secrets of God, which it is not lawful for man to speak, are not said to have ascended, but to have been taken up. This is what St. Paul clearly reveals about himself when he says, "I was taken up into paradise and heard secret words which it is not granted to any man to utter."[20]

Now, the book of Wisdom teaches us that by the works of God (namely his creation), a man may ascend unto the knowledge and love of the Creator,[21] as well as the Apostle,[22] not to mention reason itself, since the efficient cause may be known by the effects, and the example by the image. There can be no doubt that all creatures are the works of God, and Holy Scripture teaches that man and angels are not only his works, but also images of God.

So, being moved by these reasons, I now make use of the small rest from public business, as well as being admonished by the example of St. Bonaventure, who wrote *On the*

---

[19] Ps. 83 (84):8.

[20] 2 Cor. 12:4.

[21] Wis. 13:4-5 *et seq.*

[22] Rom. 1:20.

AUTHOR'S PREFACE

Journey of the Mind to God during a similar period of rest, I have attempted to set up a ladder from the consideration of creation, whereby one may in some way ascend unto God. Now, I have divided the work into fifteen steps, in resemblance of the fifteen steps whereby they went up into the Temple of Solomon, and of the fifteen Psalms which are called *Graduales*.[23]

---

[23] There is a double meaning here that is lost in English. In Latin, the root of *graduales* is *gradus*, which means a step, and Bellarmine evokes the steps of a ladder with the etymology of the name of these Psalms.

THE LADDER OF ASCENT UNTO GOD

THE LADDER OF ASCENT
UNTO GOD

THE FIRST STEP
From the Consideration of Man

CHAPTER I
The Common Causes of this Consideration

F anyone would truly desire to set up a ladder unto God, he should begin from the consideration of himself. For every one of us is both the creature and image of God, and nothing is nearer to us than ourselves. Thus, it is not without reason that Moses says "Attend to yourself," upon which two words St. Basil the Great wrote an excellent sermon.[1] The man that shall truly behold himself and consider what is within him, will find, as it were, a shortcut through the whole world, whereby he may ascend unto the Creator of all things with ease.

Now, at the present I intend to seek nothing else than the four common causes: Who is my maker? Of what matter did he make me? What form did he give me? And to what end did he produce me? For if I seek my Maker, I will find God alone; if I seek the matter whereof he made me, I shall find altogether nothing. From there I gather, that whatsoever is in me was made by God, and the whole is of God. If I seek my form, I shall find myself to be in the image of God; if I seek my end, I shall find that the same God is my supreme and total happiness. As a result, I shall understand that there is so great a connection and proximity of myself

---

[1] *Hom. III*, on the word, *Attend to yourself,* (πρόεχε σεαυτῷ in LXX).

with God, that he is my sole maker, author, and Father, my example, my happiness, and my *all*. Then, if I understand this, how could it be that I should do anything but seek him most ardently, to think of him, sigh for him, desire to see and embrace him? And to detect that blindness of my heart which for so long a time has desired, sought, or thought of nothing less than of God, who is alone the *all* unto me?

Chapter II
God our Creator

Now, let us more diligently consider everything in particular. I ask you, O my soul, who caused you to exist when, a little while ago you were nothing? Certainly the parents of your flesh did not beget you, because what is born of flesh is flesh,[2] but you are spirit. Neither heaven, nor the earth, nor the sun and stars produced you, since they are bodies, and you do not have a body. Nor yet could angels, archangels, or any other spiritual creature be the cause of your existence, because you are not made of any matter, rather, you were created out of nothing. None but God, however, can make something from nothing.

He alone, without companion, without help, with his own hands, which are his understanding and will, created you at his pleasure. Now, perhaps God himself did not produce your body, rather created things produced it so that as your soul must acknowledge God, so your body must acknowledge your parents as authors. It is not so, for although God employs parents to beget the flesh, as inferior workmen in the building of a house, yet he is the principal builder, author, and true Father both of the soul and body,

---

[2] John 3:6.

and so would be said to be the architect of man's whole being. If, however, the parents of your flesh were the true authors, and as it were, the principal architects, they would know how many muscles, veins, sinews, bones, how many humors, how many joints and many other things of this sort which there are in man's body, all of which they are ignorant of unless they might have learned them from the art of anatomy.

Besides, when the body is sick, or a member withered or cut off, they could certainly repair it again by the same skill from which they made it if they were the true authors, in the same way that craftsman who make clocks or houses know how to repair them. Parents, however, do not know how to do any of these things. Additionally, the union of the soul with the body, which is a particular part of the efficient cause of man's nature, cannot be done by any workman, except one of infinite power. By what craft except the divine can a spirit be joined with the flesh in so close a bond as to be made one substance? The body has no proportion or likeness with the spirit. Thus, he did it, "Who alone does great wonders."[3]

So truly, the spirit of the Lord spoke through Moses in Deuteronomy: "Is not he your father, that possessed you and made you and created you?"[4] And through Job, "You have clothed me with skin and flesh, you have put me together with bones and sinews."[5] And again by the kingly prophet: "Your hands have made me and formed me,"[6] and "You have formed me and laid your hand upon me."[7] And the wisest mother of the Maccabee children, "I know not how you were formed in my womb; for I neither gave you breath, nor soul,

---

[3] Ps. 135 (136):4.
[4] Deut. 32:6.
[5] Job 10:11.
[6] Ps. 118 (119):73.
[7] Ps. 138 (139):5.

nor life; nor did I frame the limbs of every one of you. But the Creator of the world that formed the birth of man and that found out the origin of all."[8]

Hence, surely the wisdom of God, Christ our Lord said, "Call no man your father upon earth; for one is your father who is in heaven."[9] By such an admonition, St. Augustine said to God of his own son Adeodatus, whom he had begot in fornication, "You did make him well, but I, beside sin, had nothing in that child."[10]

Well now, my soul, if God is your author as well as of your body, if he is your father, steward, and nurse, if what you are is of him, if what you have you received is from him, and you await what you hope for from him, why do you not boast in such a parent? Why do you not love him with all your heart? Why do you not scorn all earthly things for his sake? Why do you suffer vain desires to overrule you? Lift up your eyes to him, fear not your enemies on earth, since you have an almighty father in heaven. With what confidence and affection do you suppose David had when he said, "I am yours, save me?"[11] O my soul, if you were just to think of the fact that the almighty and everlasting God, who wants none of your goods, and if you perish loses nothing, does not turn his eyes from you, but so loves, protects, directs, and cherishes you, as if you were his great treasure, then surely you would only hope in him! You would fear him as your Lord, and love him as your Father; nor would any great temporal good or evil separate you from his love.

---

[8] 2 Mach. 7:22-23.
[9] Matt. 23:9.
[10] *Confess.* 9, 6.
[11] Ps. 118 (119):94.

CHAPTER III
God has Created Man Out of Nothing

LET US come to the matter from which man was formed. Truly it is the lowliest substance, but the more lowly it is, the more suitable it becomes to form in us the virtue of humility, by which virtue nothing in this life is more precious, and rarer, and thereby more precious and to be sought after with greater desire.

Without a doubt, nothing can be conceived which is lowlier and emptier than the material of our body, which is nothing of itself. What is the material of the body nearer to than menstrual blood? A thing so foul that our eyes recoil from it, our hands refuse to touch it, and our minds shudder to think of it. The matter from which the first man was made, what was it but red and barren earth, or dust and slime? "The Lord God formed man of the slime of the earth."[12] Again, God said to man: "You are dust, and to dust you shall return."[13] This is why the Patriarch Abraham, remembering his unworthiness, said to God, "Seeing I have once begun, I will speak to my Lord, whereas I am dust and ashes."[14] Yet there is no end of the vileness of this matter, for that dust or slime proceeded not from another matter, but from nothing. In the beginning God created heaven and earth, and certainly not of another heaven or earth, but nothing, so that whether we consider the soul or body, it is reduced to nothing, from where this proud creature man proceeded. Therefore, he has nothing to boast of except what he received from God. Truly, the works of man, which

---

[12] Gen. 2:7.
[13] Gen. 3:19.
[14] Gen. 28:27.

come about either from his cleverness or labor, have always something of themselves whereby, if they had understanding, they might boast against their maker. Accordingly, a golden vessel, a wooden box, an ivory or marble house, if they could speak, would indeed say to their maker, "I owe my form to you, but not the matter, and what I have of myself is more precious than what I received from you. But a man, who has altogether nothing of himself nor is anything of himself, can boast of nothing." So the Apostle speaks very truly: "If any man thinks himself to be something, whereas he is nothing, he deceives himself."[15] St. Cyprian agrees when he says, "We must glory in nothing, since nothing is ours."[16] Now you will say, men do many worthy works for which they are rightly praised, that virtue so praised may increase. It is so, but let the glory be to God, not to themselves, as it is written, "He that glories, let him glory in the Lord,"[17] and "In the Lord shall my soul be praised."[18] I ask, when a man does some excellent work, of what material does he make it? By what strength, and by whose direction and help does he do it? Surely, of a material which God and not man created, and by that strength which God gave to him, and not he to himself. He does it by God's direction and help, without which man could do no good. As it is said in the second Council of Orange, "God does many good things in man without man; but man does no good which God does not cause man to do."[19] Therefore, God deigned to use the ministry of man in doing good, which he could do by himself, that man would thereby acknowledge himself more indebted unto God, and not be proud of himself, rather, to boast in the Lord.[20]

---

[15] Gal. 6:3.
[16] *Testimonia ad Quirin.* 3,4.
[17] 2 Cor. 10:17.
[18] Ps. 33:3.
[19] Conc. Arausic. (529), can. 20.
[20] Wis. 10:12-20.

So my soul, if you are wise, always sit in the lowest place; do not steal God's glory, neither in little nor in much; descend to your nothingness, which is yours alone, and all the world cannot make you proud. Now, because this precious virtue of humility was almost gone out of the world, and not to be found either in the books of philosophers or in the manners of the peoples; the master of humility came from heaven, and "Who being in the form of God, emptied himself, taking the form of a servant, and humbled himself, becoming obedient unto death."[21] Then to mankind he said, "Learn of me because I am meek and humble of heart, and you shall find rest to your souls."[22] This is why, my soul, if you are perchance ashamed to imitate the humility of man, do not be ashamed to imitate the humility of God, who does not deceive you, nor can be deceived, and who resists the proud and gives grace to the humble.[23]

Chapter IV
Man Was Created in the Image of God

IT FOLLOWS that we consider the form which is the third cause. Now truly, the lowlier the matter is from which man was made, so much more precious and excellent is the form which was given to him. I pass over the exterior form of the body, i.e. the figure of the human body, which is more excellent than the figures of all animals. This form is not substantial, but accidental. Thus, the substantial form of man, namely what makes him man, is what distinguishes him from other living creatures. This is his immortal soul, endowed with reason and free will, which is God's Image,

---

[21] Phil. 2:6-8.
[22] Matt. 11:29.
[23] Jas 4:6.

made to his own likeness.

We read that when God made man he said, "Let us make man to our image and likeness; and let him have dominion over the fishes of the sea, and the birds of the air, and the beasts, and the whole earth, and every creeping creature that moves upon the earth."[24] Thus, man is God's image, not because of his body, but of his soul; God is a spirit, not a body, and as St. Basil says, "Wherever there is one with command over other living creatures there is the image of God."[25] Now, man does not command the beasts by the members of the body, which are stronger in many beasts than in man, but by his mind endowed with reason and freewill. For, he does not rule them by what he has in common with them, but by that whereby he is distinguished from them and made like unto God.

Raise your mind, O my soul, to your example, and consider that all the good of an image has been posited in the similitude it bears to its example. If perhaps the example is deformed (as the devil is usually depicted), then the good of the image is suitably to represent its deformed example. Therefore, deformity in example shall still be deformity, but in the image it will be beauty. Then, if the example will also be beautiful, the image will be most precious, if, as much as it can, it imitates the beauty of the example. Likewise, the image, if it had understanding, would desire nothing more than to behold continually the example, to fashion and frame itself to become as much like it as possible.

Your example, O my soul, is God, an infinite beauty, a light in which there is no darkness,[26] whose beauty the sun and moon admire. To imitate an example of such beauty more easily and desire as much as you can to be like him, wherein consists your supreme perfection, profit, honor, joy,

---

[24] Gen. 1:26.
[25] *Hexaemeron*, 10.
[26] 1 Jn. 1:5.

The First Step: The Consideration of Man

rest, and happiness; consider that the beauty of God, your example, consists in wisdom and holiness. The way in which the beauty of the body arises from proportion of its members and an amiable color, so in the beauty of the mind, an amiable color is the light of wisdom, and the proportion of members is justice; but by justice no particular virtue is understood, rather, that universal one which contains every virtue. Thus, that soul is most beautiful whose mind shines with the light of wisdom, and whose will is confirmed in the fullness of perfect justice. Now, O my soul, I say that God your example is Wisdom and Justice, and so beauty itself. Since this twofold goodness is signified by the name of holiness in the Scriptures, therefore, in Isaiah the angels cry unto God, "Holy, Holy, Holy, the Lord God of hosts."[27] God himself also cries unto his images, "I am the Lord your God. Be holy, because I am holy."[28] Then our Lord in the Gospel, "Be you therefore perfect, as also your heavenly Father is perfect."[29]

So if you desire, O my soul, as the true image of God, to be as like to your example as you possibly can, it behooves you to love wisdom and justice before all things. It is true wisdom to judge all things according to the highest cause; the highest cause is the will of God, or the law which makes known the will of God unto men. As a result, if you love wisdom, you must not have any care for what the law of the flesh teaches, what the senses esteem, what the world approves, what your relatives persuade, and much less what flatterers propound. Be deaf to them all, and only attend the will of your Lord God, and you will judge on every side that to be wholly good, profitable, glorious and desirable, which is in conformity to the will and law of God. This is the wisdom of the saints of which the wise man writes, "I loved

---

[27] Isa. 6:3.
[28] Lev. 11:44.
[29] Matt. 5:48.

her above health and beauty, and chose to have her instead of light; for her light cannot be put out. Now all good things came to me together with her."[30]

Moreover justice is another part of spiritual beauty, and embraces all the virtues which adorn and perfect the will, but especially charity, the mother and root of all virtues. St. Augustine speaks of this in his book *On Nature and Grace*, "Imperfect charity is imperfect justice; charity increased is justice increased; perfect charity is perfect justice."[31] For, "he that loves has fulfilled the law," because, "love works no evil", and therefore, "love is the fulfilling of the law."[32]

Again, "he that keeps his word," i.e., his commandments, "in him indeed the charity of God has been perfected."[33] So those who will be like the divine example, ought to obey the one who says, "Be therefore followers of God, as most dear children, and walk in love."[34]

Oh my soul, if you were to understand these things clearly, and be like your example in beauty of true wisdom and justice, then you would please the eyes of the most high king; what great peace you would then enjoy! How you would rejoice! How quickly would you scorn all worldly delights! Conversely, if you would consider how greatly God is offended to see his image destitute of the light of wisdom and beauty of justice, polluted, defiled and darkened, and man that was placed in such honor as to be like unto God, "now to be compared to senseless beasts and become like them,"[35] then you surely could not do anything but shudder and tremble in horror, until you washed away all your stains with floods of tears flowing from deep contrition. In this way, you will quickly return to the likeness of your most

---

[30] Wis. 7:10-11.
[31] *De Natura et Gratia*, c. 70 n. 84.
[32] Rom. 13:8, 10.
[33] 1 John 2:5.
[34] Eph. 5:1-2.
[35] Ps. 48 (49):13.

beautiful example. Yet, because while you are a pilgrim on earth, and "walk by faith and not by sight,"[36] you continually want the help of your Lord God, as well to remain in the likeness you already have, as also daily to become more like, i.e., more bright and beautiful. Sigh, therefore, from the bottom of your heart to God, and say unto him: O holy and most merciful Lord, whom it has pleased to make this my soul your own image, make perfect, I beg you, that your said image increase in it wisdom and justice, hide it in your secret tabernacle, that it would not be defiled with the slime of carnal concupiscence, with the smoke of worldly honor or the dust of earthly thoughts.

CHAPTER V
The Beatific Vision of God Is the Intrinsic End of Man

THERE remains the last cause, which is the end. The end wherefore man was created is none other than God himself. Yet, because the end is twofold, the one intrinsical, the other external, let us briefly consider each of them apart. The intrinsic end of everything is the perfect state to which a thing can arrive at. The intrinsic end of a palace is the perfect finishing of it; for then it is said to be ended, when nothing proper to the building is wanting. The intrinsic end of a tree is the most perfect state which its nature requires; for then a tree may be said to have attained its end when it spreads the boughs, brings forth leaves, is beautified with blossoms, and soon after is loaded with ripe fruit. So man, who was created for the loftiest end, may thus also be said to have attained his end when his mind shall see God just as he is, and in him know all things, his will shall enjoy the

---

[36] 2 Cor. 5:7.

chief happiness most ardently loved, and his body qualified with the glorious gifts of immortality, impassibility, and the like, shall obtain perpetual rest and joy. And because the sight of God is the essence of this final beatitude whereby we who are the images of God must obtain a most perfect estate by the resemblance of our divine example, so St. John writes, "We are now the sons of God, and it has not yet appeared what we shall be. We know that when he shall appear we shall be like to him, because we shall see him as he is."[37]

If you could imagine, O my soul, what this means, "we shall be like to him, because we shall see him as he is," how soon would all the clouds of earthly thoughts be dispersed! God is most happy, and therefore most happy because he always beholds himself as he is, and enjoys himself most clearly seen and most ardently loved from all eternity. He would have you also partake of this inestimable good with the angels; he created you for this most high and happy end. That saying, "enter into the joy of your Lord,"[38] signifies this: be a partaker of the joy which God himself enjoys, and again: "I dispose to you, as my Father has disposed to me, a kingdom, that you may eat and drink at my table in my kingdom,"[39] i.e., I make you partakers of my kingdom and kingly table, that you may enjoy that honor, power and pleasure, which I and God my Father enjoy. Who is able to conceive what is the honor, power, pleasure, and happiness of the king of all kings, and the lord of all lords, the Lord our God? Certainly, if any would but in thought and hope ascend unto so great a loftiness of our end, he would be ashamed to contend for the possession of this earth, to grieve for any temporal loss, or to rejoice in any temporal gain; he would be ashamed, I say, to partake in the pleasures

---

[37] 1 John 3:2.
[38] Matt. 25:21.
[39] Lk 22:29-30.

which beasts desire, who has become a companion of the Angels, and a partaker of God's friendship and of his inestimable delights; for all things among friends are common.

Chapter VI
The Glory of God and His Own Eternal Salvation Is the Extrinsic End of Man

NOW, the external end of everything is that for which it is made. The end of a palace is the dweller therein; the end of a tree is the possessor thereof; the end of man is only his Lord God, for of himself and for himself he made man, and he keeps, feeds, and pays him his wages. Therefore, he justly commands and says, "You shall fear the Lord your God, and him alone shall you serve." Now, mark with all care, O my soul, the things which are made for man are profitable to man, and not to themselves; beasts labor for man and not for themselves, the fields, vineyards and orchards fill the granaries, cellars, and purses of men; neither do servants labor, sweat and toil for themselves, but for the profit, ease and pleasure of their masters. But your Lord God, who wants nothing, would have man truly serve him, and yet the profit and reward of his service he will not have.

"For you, O Lord, are sweet and mild; and plenteous in mercy,"[40] who would not serve you with all his heart if once he began to taste a little the sweetness of your rule? What, O Lord, do you command your servants? "Take my yoke upon you." And what is your yoke? "My yoke is sweet and my burden light."[41] Who would not most joyfully carry a

---

[40] Deut. 6:13.
[41] Matt. 11:29, 30.

yoke that does not punish but comfort, and a burden that does not wear but refresh? Therefore, it is not without cause that he adds, "and you shall find rest for your souls." What is your yoke which does not cause fatigue, but grants rest? Namely, that first and greatest commandment, "You shall love the Lord your God with your whole heart."[42] What is easier, more pleasant and delightful than to love goodness, beauty and excellence itself, which you are, O my Lord God? your servant David judged right who esteemed your commandments, "More to be desired than gold and many precious stones, and sweeter than honey and the honeycomb," and he added, "and in keeping them there is a great reward."[43] What does this mean, O Lord? Do you promise a reward to those that keep your commandments "more to be desired than gold and sweeter than the honeycomb?" Yes, truly, you promise a most ample reward, as James your Apostle says, "God has promised the crown of life to them that love him."[44] What is a crown of life? Truly a greater happiness than we are able to conceive. For St. Paul speaks this way from Isaiah: "Eye has not seen, nor ear heard, neither has it entered into the heart of man, what things God has prepared for them that love him."[45] Surely, therefore, there is great reward for keeping your commandments. That first and greatest commandment is not only profitable to the obedient man, and not God the lawgiver, but also the rest of God's commandments do perfect, beautify, instruct, and illuminate the obedient, and finally, make them good and happy. Therefore, if you are wise, understand that you were created for God's glory and your eternal salvation. This is your end, this center of your soul, this treasure of your heart. If you come to that end, you

---

[42] Matt. 22:37.
[43] Ps. 18 (19):11, 12.
[44] Jas 1:12.
[45] 1 Cor. 2:9, cf. Isa. 44:4.

will be happy; if you turn away from it, you will be unhappy. Therefore, consider what directs you to that end assuredly good, and assuredly evil what causes you to turn away from it. Prosperity and adversity, wealth and poverty, health and sickness, honor and ignominy, life and death of a wise man are neither to be desired nor avoided; but if they bestow God's glory and your eternal welfare, they are good and to be desired; if they hinder it, they are evil and to be avoided.

THE SECOND STEP
From the Consideration of the Greater World

Chapter I
The Greatness of the World and the Greatness of God

E have constructed the first step of our ladder of ascension unto God from the consideration of man, who is called the lesser world. Now, we also intend to frame the second step from the consideration of this very great corporeal quantity, commonly called the greater world. St. Gregory Nazianzen writes in his *Second Sermon of Easter*, that God placed man as a great world in a lesser world; which is true if we separate angels from the world. Man is greater than the whole corporeal world, not in quantity, but in quality; but if it be that angels are understood in the world, as we in this place understand them, then man is a lesser world placed in a greater world. In this greater world, therefore, which contains all things, many things are to be wondered at, but especially quantity, multitude, variety, efficacy, and beauty. All of which, if they are attentively considered with God's illumination and assistance, they have great force to elevate the mind in such a way, that in admiration of a certain immense magnitude, multitude, variety, efficaciousness and beauty, it would faint, as it were, and being returned to itself, whatsoever it beholds without God, it will despise as vain and empty.

Truly, the earth is so great that Sirach says, "Who has

measured the breadth of the earth and the depth of the abyss?"[1] This may also be understood that in so many thousand years as have passed since the creation, as yet the whole surface of the earth (for that Sirach called the breadth of the earth) is not even known to us, who daily have sought after it. And what, I ask, is the greatness of the earth compared to the compass of the highest heaven? Not without reason do astronomers say it is a point. For we see the sun beams, so to illuminate the opposite stars of the firmament, although the earth be between, as if the same were nothing at all. And if every star in the firmament is greater than the whole earth (as the common opinion of wise men is), and yet seem to us, because of their almost infinite distance, to be very small, who then can conceive the greatness of heaven in which so many million stars shine? So if Sirach said, "Who has measured the breadth of the earth and the depth of the abyss," what would he have said of the compass of the highest heaven, and distance thereof unto the lowest hell? Truly it is so great that it cannot be imagined. Well now my soul, I ask you, if the world is so great, how great is he that made the world? "Great is the Lord, and of his greatness there is no end."[2] Hear Isaiah: "Who has measured the waters in the hollow of his hand, and weighed the heavens with his palm? Who has poised with three fingers the bulk of the earth?"[3] St. Jerome says, according to the edition of Aquila, by *pugillum* is understood "little finger,"[4] so that the sense is: the whole element of water, which is less than the earth, is measured with one little finger of God; the earth with three fingers, the heaven (which is greater than the earth and water together) is weighed with a span. But this is spoken

---

[1] Sirach 1:2.
[2] Ps. 144 (145):3.
[3] Isa. 40:12.
[4] St. Jerome, *Commentary on Isaiah* 40:40, n. 487: *Quis mensus est pugillo aquas*, etc.

metaphorically, for God is a spirit, and has no hands nor fingers properly; and the Scripture sufficiently shows by these comparisons that God is much greater than his creatures, which Solomon indicated more expressly when he said, "Heaven and the heaven of heavens do not contain you."[5]

This is true, because if another world were created, God would also fill that, and if many other worlds, or even infinite worlds were made, God would fill them all. But do not think my soul, that your God does so fill the world that a part of God is in a part of the world, and all God in all the world; for God has no parts, but is all in all the world, and all in every part of the world. Consequently, if you are faithful to him, although armies may rise up against you, your heart shall not fear, for what should he fear who has an almighty Father, friend, and spouse, who sees all things, and loves you with a most ardent love? If for your sins you have God as an angry judge and an almighty enemy, who sees all things, and with implacable hatred hating all sins, then you have just cause to dread with horrible fear, and to give your eyes and feet no rest, until God has been pleased with your repentance, you take breath in the light of his mercies.

Chapter II
The Multitude of Things Created and the Infinity of the Perfection of the Creator

MOREOVER, who can number the multitude of things created by one God, maker of heaven and earth? Sirach says, "Who has numbered the sand of the sea and the drops of the

---

[5] 2 Chron. 6:18.

rain?"[6] How many metals of gold and silver, brass, lead, precious stones, gems, and pearls are there within the earth and sea? How many kinds and types of herbs, fruits, and plants are there upon the earth? Furthermore, how many species of perfect or imperfect living creatures, four-footed beasts, insects and birds? How many kinds and genuses of fish in the sea? Who can number them? What of the multitude of mankind, of whom it is written, "according to your highness you have multiplied the children of men."[7] How many stars also are there in heaven, and angels above heaven? Of the stars we read in the most true Scripture: "Number the stars if you can."[8] In another place also, they are compared to the sands of the sea, which are innumerable.[9] Of the angels, Daniel writes, "thousands of thousands ministered to him, and ten thousand times a hundred thousand stood before him."[10] And St. Thomas affirms, with St. Dionysius, that the multitude of angels exceeds in number all material things.[11] Consequently, this almost infinite multitude of things made by one God demonstrates that in the divine essence there are infinite perfections. For God would be known to man in some sort by his creatures; because no creature can truly represent the infinite perfection of the Creator, he has multiplied the creatures and has given to every one some goodness and perfection. Thereby it is gathered from the goodness and perfection of the Creator, who in our most simple essence includes infinite perfections, even after a sort as one piece of gold contains the value of many pieces of brass.

Therefore, my soul, whatever you see or imagine which seems admirable to you, let it be a ladder to ascend to the

---

[6] Sirach 1:2.
[7] Ps. 11(12):9.
[8] Gen. 15:5.
[9] Jer. 33:22.
[10] Dan. 7:10.
[11] St. Thomas, *Summa* I, q. 1 art. 3; Dionysius Areop. *Hierarch. Coelest.*, c. 4.

knowledge of your Creator, who without a doubt is greater and more wonderful. So it will happen, that created things which "are turned to a snare to the feet of the universe,"[12] as Wisdom teaches, will instruct, not deceive, and direct not misguide you from the way of virtue. So if you possess gold, silver, and precious stones, say in your heart, my God is more precious who has promised me himself, if I scorn these things. If you admire earthly empires and kingdoms, say in your heart, how much more excellent is the kingdom of heaven which remains forever, which God, who does not lie, has promised to those that love him. If pleasures and delights begin to tickle your carnal senses, then say in your heart: the pleasure of the spirit is more delightful than of the flesh, and the delights of the mind surpass those of the belly, for the mortal creature offers the latter, and the immortal Creator the former, and anyone that tastes them may say with the Apostle: "I am filled with comfort; I exceedingly abound with joy in all our tribulation."[13] Lastly, if any beautiful, great or wonderful thing were to be offered to you beside your Lord God, answer assuredly: whatever goodness is in it, the same is certainly much greater and better in your Lord. Thus, it is not profitable for you to change gold for brass, precious stones for glass, great things for small, certain for doubtful, and temporal for eternal.

Chapter III
The Variety of Created Things and God as the Infinite Source of All Good

ALTHOUGH the multitude of creatures is admirable, and

---

[12] Wis. 14:11.
[13] 2 Cor 7:4.

proves the manifold perfections of our God, yet more admirable is the variety of things which is seen in that multiplication. It is not hard, with one seal to express many figures alike, or with the same font to print innumerable letters; but to distinguish the former's most infinite ways, as God did in the creation, is plainly a divine work, most worthy of admiration. I will pass over the kinds and types of things which are constituted of very great differences. How great a variety is there in the particulars of herbs, plants, flowers and fruits! Their figures, colors, odors, tastes, how wonderfully distinguished! Are not the like also in living creatures that have sense? What will I say of men, since in a large army there can hardly be found two men alike. Such a thing is also found in the stars and the angels, "For one star differs from another in brightness,"[14] as the Apostle witnesses. St. Thomas also says that angels, although they exceed corporeal things in number, yet they all differ among themselves, not only in individual number, but also in their specific form.[15]

Now my soul, lift up your eyes to God, in whom are the causes of all things, and from whom, as from a fountain of infinite abundance, this almost infinite variety flowed. For God could not have imprinted those innumerable forms in creatures, without containing their causes in the bosom of his essence after a most high and eminent manner. Not without reason then does the Apostle cry out, "O the depth of the riches of the wisdom and of the knowledge of God."[16] Truly, it is a well of infinite depth, in which the treasures of wisdom and knowledge are hidden, which could beget such a variety of things. Rightly did St. Francis say unto God: "My God and my all," since whatever goodness which has been divided and distributed among creatures, is found united in

---

[14] 1 Cor. 15:41.
[15] *loc. cit.* art. 4.
[16] Rom. 11:33.

The Second Step: The Greater World

God by a certain better and higher way. But you will say, O my soul, although these things seem to be true, yet creatures we see, we touch, we taste, and really enjoy; but God we cannot see, touch, taste, enjoy, nor scarcely conceive, but as a thing very far from us; as a result, little wonder if created things affect us more than God. Now, if you are strong in faith, my soul, and continue in hope as well as charity, you cannot deny but that after this life, which vanishes like a shadow, you will see God as he is in himself, and enjoy him much more inwardly than you enjoy creatures now. Hear our redeemer: "Blessed are the clean of heart, for they shall see God,"[17] and St. Paul, "We see now by a glass darkly, but then face to face,"[18] and St. John, "We shall be like unto him, because we shall see him as he is."[19] Moreover, how much of the world belongs to you? Truly, neither the whole nor the half, nor a third or fourth, nor scarce a small portion thereof falls to your share, which in a short time you must be constrained to forsake. But God, in whom all things are, you shall enjoy for all eternity; "God shall be all in all,"[20] in his saints, and blessed without end. He shall be your life, food, clothing, home, honor, wealth, pleasure, and your all. Furthermore, your sweet and merciful God does not command you to want altogether the solace of his creatures while you are a pilgrim on earth, for he made them all to serve you. Rather, he commands you to use them soberly and moderately, and give joyfully of your store to the needy, having dominion over your wealth in using it to the glory of God. So weigh very carefully if it would not be more expedient for you to lack the created things in this life even as they are necessary, and in the other, to enjoy your Creator eternally, in whom all things are; or on the other

---

[17] Matt. 5:8.
[18] 1 Cor. 13:12.
[19] 1 Jn. 3:2.
[20] 1 Cor. 15:28.

hand, to labor in earnest in this life to purchase temporal goods, and never to be satisfied with their plenty, but then in the other, to be deprived both of temporal and eternal. Additionally, God is never far from those that love him, since even in this life he gives them greater delights than the lovers of the world find in creatures. It is not falsely written, "I have been mindful of God and am delighted,"[21] and "be delighted in our Lord, and he will give you the petitions of your heart,"[22] and, "I truly will be delighted in our Lord,"[23] and, "Make the soul of your servant rejoice, because to you, O Lord, have I lifted up my soul."[24] To omit the rest, where the Apostle said, "I am replenished with consolation, I do exceedingly abound in joy in all our tribulations,"[25] truly he does not mean that consolation comes from tribulation, or joy from sorrow, for "thorns do not bring forth grapes, nor brambles figs,"[26] but that to mitigate tribulations, God always sends to his friends such pure, clear, and solid comforts, that temporal joys may not in any sort be compared to them. So, my soul, let this be with you a sure conclusion: the man who finds God, finds all; the man who loses God, loses all.

Chapter IV
The Inherent Virtue in Created Things, and the Omnipotence of God

IT FOLLOWS now that from the power which God has given

---

[21] Ps. 76 (77):4.
[22] Ps. 36 (37):4.
[23] Ps. 103 (104):34.
[24] Ps. 80 (81):4.
[25] 2 Cor. 7:4.
[26] Matt. 7:16.

The Second Step: The Greater World 25

to creatures, we ascend to understanding the infinite power of the Creator. There is altogether nothing which does not have in it admirable virtue, or power, or efficacy. If a stone falls from a high place, with what force does it fall? What does it not break? What can resist it? When the Holy Spirit in the Apocalypse describes the excessive violence with which the great Babylon, i.e. the whole company of the wicked, shall be cast headlong into hell on the day of judgment, he speaks in this way: "And one strong angel took up, as it were, a great millstone, and threw it into the sea, saying: With this violence shall Babylon, that great city, be thrown, and shall be found no more."[27] That water likewise, which is so smooth and soft, and runs gently over the earth; when it is angry, and swells in rivers or brooks, it bears down and destroys all things in its path, and not only farmhouses, but also the gates and walls of cities, and we have seen bridges of marble broken down by it. Moreover, the winds which blow so sweetly, sometimes beat great ships against the rocks, and overturn ancient oak trees. I myself have seen (and if I had not seen it I would not believe it) a very great heap of dirt dug up by a vehement wind, and carried upon a country village, so that a deep ditch was seen from where the dirt had been taken, and the whole village to which the dirt was carried was covered and thereby, in a manner, buried. What shall we say of fire? How quickly does a small fire become a great flame, consuming woods and houses as it were in a moment! St. James says, "Behold how a little fire kindles a great forest."[28]

What activity is there in herbs! What power in stones, and especially in lodestone and amber! Then, among beasts, some we see are very strong, such as lions, bears, bulls, and elephants, while others are very clever although very small such as ants, spiders, bees, etc., let alone the power of

---
[27] Apoc. 18:21.
[28] Jas 3:5.

angels, of the sun and stars, which are far from us. How excellent is the cleverness of man, whereby so many sciences have been devised? It is such that we often doubt whether they are an art of nature, or rather more, whether it clearly surpasses nature.

Now lift up the eyes of the mind unto God, O my soul, and consider what virtue, efficacy, and power is in the Lord your God, of whom the most true Scripture says, "Who is like to you among the strong, O Lord?,"[29] and "Who alone does great marvels,"[30] and "The blessed and mighty alone, the King of Kings, and Lord of Lords."[31] For whatever power that creatures have, they received it from God and shall enjoy it so long as it pleases him. Who but God saw to it that neither the waters of the sea, nor the teeth of the whale hurt Jonah in the whale's belly?[32] Who but God shut the mouths of the hungry lions so they could not touch Daniel?[33] Who but God preserved the three children from harm in the fiery furnace?[34] Who but Christ, true God, said to the furious winds and raging sea, "Peace, be still," and the wind ceased, so there was made a great calm?[35] That God, who did not receive virtue and power from any other, but whose will is a power against which none can resist, has infinite power always and everywhere, in comparison with which all the power of men is nothing. For Isaiah speaks in this way: "All nations are before him as though they had no being; and they are reputed of him as nothing, and a vain thing."[36]

Are they not fools who fear created things and not the almighty Creator? Are they not fools who trust in their own

---

[29] Exod. 15:11.
[30] Ps. 135 (136):4.
[31] 1 Tim. 6:15.
[32] Jonah 2:1 seqq.
[33] Dan. 6:16 seq.
[34] Dan. 3:23 seq.
[35] Mk 4:39.
[36] Isa. 40:17.

strength and that of their friends, but not in God? "If God is for us, who is against us?"[37] And if God is against us, who shall be for us?

Consequently, O my soul, if you are wise, "be humbled under the mighty hand of God."[38] Love him truly, and you will not need to fear what man or devil, or any creature can do to you. If perhaps, you have fallen, and provoked your God to anger, give your head no rest until you are at peace with him, "for it is horrible to fall into the hands of the living God."[39]

Chapter V
The Created Beauty of Things, and the Uncreated Beauty of God

IT REMAINS that we consider the beauty of creatures, whereof the prophet said: "You have delighted me, O Lord, in what you have made."[40] Now truly, as all things that God made are good, so are they all beautiful, if they are considered rightly. Now, omitting the rest, let us speak of what in the judgment and opinion of all men are beautiful. Surely, there is great beauty in a green meadow, in a well kept garden, a pleasant forest, a calm sea, clear air, fountains, rivers, cities, and of the bright sky garnished with numberless stars, like gems. What a delight to us is the beauty of a tree clothed with blossoms or loaded with fruit; the shapes likewise of different kinds of four-footed beasts, the flight of birds, and the playing of fishes! What shall I say of the beauty of the moon and stars, but especially of the great and bright radiance of the sun, which gladdens all the world by its rising? But men to whom we chiefly speak, are delighted

---

[37] Rom. 8:31.
[38] 1 Pet. 5:6.
[39] Ps. 91 (92):5.
[40] Ps. 91 (92):5.

with nothing more than with their own beauty and comeliness. "By the beauty of women many have perished."[41] We have often seen and grieved that men, otherwise very wise, have been so in love with the beauty of women; and likewise great and honorable women brought to such folly by the beauty of men, as they have preferred their love before their state and dignity, children and parents, and even their life and eternal salvation; I add they esteem eternal salvation less than the love of beautiful men. We are acquainted with the lives of David, Solomon, and Sampson from reading the holy Scriptures, which are full of histories of similar examples.

Now my soul, if God gives so great a beauty to creatures, how great and admirable do you think is the beauty of God himself? No one can give what they do not have. If men, delighted with the beauty of the sun and stars, thought those bright bodies, says the wise man, to be gods, let them know, "how much the Lord of them is more beautiful than they, for the author of beauty made all these things."[42] We may gather how great the beauty of God is not only since it contains the beauty of all creatures most eminently within itself, but also since being invisible to us while we are pilgrims on this earth, it is only understood by the faith of the Scriptures and mirror of creatures. Just the same, many saints have been so inflamed with the love thereof, that some of them have hid themselves in deserts, and attended only to its contemplation, as St. Mary Magdalen, St. Paul the first hermit, the great St. Anthony, and others, of whom you may read in the religious history of Theodoret. Others, forsaking their wives and children and whatsoever else they possessed on earth, lived in the monasteries, under the obedience of others to enjoy the friendship of God. Others desired willingly with rigorous pains to end their lives to

---

[41] Sirach 9:9.
[42] Wis. 13:3.

come to the sight of that infinite beauty. Let us hear the Holy Martyr Ignatius in his epistle to the Romans: "Let fire, gallows, beasts, breaking of my bones, quartering of my members, bruising of my body, and all the torments of the devil come upon me, so that I may enjoy Christ."[43] So, if this divine beauty as yet unseen, but only believed and hoped for, could kindle such a fervent desire, what will it do after the veil has been removed, and it is seen as it truly is? It will doubtless bring to pass, "that being drunk with the torrent of that pleasure,"[44] we neither will nor can turn our eyes from it for a moment. And what wonder is it, if the angels and blessed souls which always see the face of their Father in heaven are not wearied or tired with that sight, since God himself, beholding his own beauty from all eternity, is fully pleased therein, and being happy by that sight, desires nothing else, entering as it were, into a vineyard or garden of all delights, from where he will never depart.

Seek that beauty, O my soul, sigh after it day and night; say with the prophet, "My soul has thirsted after the strong, living God. When shall I come and appear before the face of God?"[45] Say with the Apostle, "We are bold, and have a good will to be pilgrims rather from the body and to be present with our Lord."[46] Neither do you fear to be defiled with the love of that beauty, for the love of it comforts, rather than corrupts, purifies, rather than pollutes the heart. The holy virgin and martyr St. Agnes said truly, "I love Christ, whose Mother is a Virgin, whose Father knows no woman, whom when I love I am chaste, when I touch I am clean, when I take I remain a virgin."[47] Now, if you truly desire the uncreated beauty of your Lord, you must fulfill that which

---

[43] *Ep. Ad Rom.* 5.
[44] Ps. 25 (26):9.
[45] Ps. 41 (42):3.
[46] 2 Cor. 5:8.
[47] Prudentius, *De Coron. Hymn.* 14; Ambrose, *de Virginitate* 1, 2.

the Apostle adds in that place: "We endeavor to please him whether absent or not." If God pleases you, you should likewise please God. Surely, we will please God in the country of the living, when we shall be illuminated with his glory, as the prophet says, "I will please our Lord in the country of the living;"[48] but in this pilgrimage we are so easily polluted and defiled with the slime of sin, that the Apostle James said, "In many things we all offend,"[49] and the prophet David, to show how few are immaculate in this life, affirms that it belongs to beatitude, "Blessed are the immaculate in the way."[50] So, my soul, if you will please your Lord during pilgrimage, it is not enough to desire to please him, but it behooves you, as the Apostle says, to strive to please him; this is with great diligence to beware of such stains as may deform your face, and if any happen to stick therein, with like diligence, endeavor to wipe them away. Do you not see how women trying to please their husbands spend many hours in dressing their hair, adorning their face, and wiping away the spots of their garments; they do all this to please the eyes of a mortal man who soon after must be turned to dust and ashes! What should you do to please the eyes of your immortal spouse, who always beholds you and desires to see you without stain or wrinkle? It is needful then, to strive with all your strength, "to walk before him in holiness and justice,"[51] and hasten to remove all things that may hinder the same, not having respect for flesh and blood, nor the speeches of men; you cannot please God and the world both at once, according to the Apostle's saying: "If I did please men, I should not be the servant of Christ."[52]

---

[48] Ps. 114 (115):9.
[49] Jas 3:2.
[50] Ps. 118 (119):1.
[51] Lk. 1:75.
[52] Gal. 1:10.

THE THIRD STEP
From the Consideration of the Earth

CHAPTER I
As our Body Finds Rest upon the Earth, so in God Alone will our Mind Find Repose

E HAVE considered the corporeal world in general; let us now consider the principal parts of it, so from them we may set up our ladder for the contemplation of the Creator. First there is earth, which, although it occupies the lowest place among the elements, and seems to be less than the rest; yet it is not less than the water, and it excels the other elements in dignity and worth. Thereby we often read in Scripture that God made heaven and earth as the principal parts of the world,[1] for he made heaven as the palace of God and angels, the earth as the palace of men. "The heaven of heavens is to our Lord, but the earth he has given to the children of men."[2] That is the reason why the heaven is full of bright stars, and the earth abounds with metals, precious stones, herbs, trees, and beasts of divers kinds, whereas the water is stored only with fish, and the air and fire are in a manner empty and bare elements. Now, passing over these, the earth has three things most worthy of consideration, whereby a vigilant mind may easily ascend to God.

First, the earth is the firmest foundation of the whole world, without which we could neither walk, work, rest, nor

---

[1] Gen. 1:1; 1 Esdr. 9:6; Judith 13:24.
[2] Ps. 113 (114):25.

live. "He has established the round world which shall not be moved,"³ and "You have founded the earth upon the stability thereof, it shall not be moved forever and ever."⁴

Secondly, the earth—like a good nurse to men and other living creatures—daily brings forth fruit, grass, and innumerable things of this sort, for God speaks in this way: "Behold, I have given you all manner of herb that feeds upon the earth, and all trees that have in themselves seed of their own kind to be your meat, and to all beasts of the earth."⁵

Thirdly, the earth brings forth stones and wood to build houses, and metals of brass and iron for different uses, as well as gold and silver whereof money is made, which is the instrument whereby all things necessary for the life of man are easily procured.

Now truly, that first property of the earth, namely, to be the place in which our bodies rest, and not in the water, air, or fire, is an emblem of our Creator, in whom alone man's soul finds a place of rest. "You made us, O Lord, for yourself, and our heart is restless until it shall rest in you."⁶ Solomon, as much as any king, sought after rest in honor, wealth, and pleasure. He possessed a most ample and peaceable kingdom, so that the Scripture witnesses, "He had in his dominion all the kingdoms with him, from the river of the land of the Philistines, unto the border of Egypt; of them that offered him presents, and served him all the days of his life."⁷ his wealth also was incomparable so that he kept forty thousand horses for chariots, and twelve thousand to ride upon. And as we read in the same book, the navy of Solomon brought gold and precious stones from Ophir in such plenty that silver was worthless, and there was as

---

³ Ps. 90 (91):2.
⁴ Ps. 103 (104):5.
⁵ Gen. 1:29-30.
⁶ *Confess.* 1, 1.
⁷ 3 Kg. 4:21.

The Third Step: Consideration of the Earth 33

much in Jerusalem that there were stones in the streets. So many also were the pleasures which he had provided for himself, that they may seem incredible. For falling into the inordinate love of women, he took "seven hundred wives as queens, and concubines three hundred."[8] But let us hear him speak of himself in Ecclesiastes:

> I made me great works, I built me houses, and planted vineyards,
>
> I made gardens, and orchards, and set them with trees of all kinds,
>
> And I made me ponds of water, to water therewith the wood of the young trees,
>
> I got me menservants, and maidservants, and had a great family: and herds of oxen, and great flocks of sheep, above all that were before me in Jerusalem:
>
> I heaped together for myself silver and gold, and the wealth of kings, and provinces: I made me singing men, and singing women, and the delights of the sons of men, cups and vessels to serve to pour out wine:
>
> And I surpassed in riches all that were before me in Jerusalem: my wisdom also remained with me.
>
> And whatsoever my eyes desired, I refused them not: and I withheld not my heart from enjoying every pleasure, and delighting itself in the things which I had prepared: and esteemed this my portion, to make use of my own labor.[9]

Thus he who doubtless had as great a scorn as could be had in creatures, for he neither wanted kingdoms nor wealth, nor pleasures, nor so much as esteemed human wisdom, and lastly he enjoyed peace a long time to possess such great happiness.

Let us see now if all these things could content and satisfy the desires of his mind:

> And when I turned myself to all the works which my

---

[8] 3 Kg. 11:3.
[9] 2:40-10

hands had wrought, and to the labors wherein I had labored in vain, I saw in all things vanity, and vexation of mind, and that nothing was lasting under the sun.[10]

Solomon, therefore, did not find rest in all of his riches, delights, wisdom, and honors; nor could he, although he had enjoyed much more, for the soul of man is immortal, and these things are mortal, and cannot long remain under the sun, neither can it be that a soul which is capable of infinite good should be satisfied with finite goods. Therefore, as the body of man cannot rest in the air, although it is very spacious, nor in the water, though it is deep, because the earth is his center, and not the air or water, so the mind of man is never satisfied with airy dignities, nor muddy and watery wealth, namely with soft and deceiving pleasures, and not with the false glory of human knowledge, but with God alone, who is the center of souls and their only true place of rest.

O how truly and wisely did the father of Solomon say: "What is mine in heaven, and what would I want upon the earth but you? O God of my heart and God my portion forever."[11] In other words: I find nothing in heaven or earth or in any creature therein that can give me true contentment, you alone are the God of my heart, that is, you alone are a firm rock to my heart; for the word "God" in the Hebrew text means a rock in that place. You, therefore, are only a most firm rock to my heart, in you alone I will rest, you alone are my portion, my inheritance, and all my good; other things are nothing, nor of any force to suffice for me a day, but you alone will suffice for me forever.

Do you yet understand, O my soul, that God alone is the rock whereupon you must rest? In everything else there is vanity and affliction of spirit, because they do not have existence, but merely the appearance of it; they do not

---

[10] Eccl. 2:11.
[11] Ps. 72 (73):25-26.

comfort you, rather they afflict, because they are obtained with labor, kept with fear, and lost with sorrow. So despise all transitory things, if you are wise, lest they carry you away with them; and abide in that unity and bond of charity which continues forever. Lift up your heart to God in heaven, lest it putrefy on earth, and learn true wisdom from the folly of many, in whose names the wise man speaks, saying:

> Therefore we have erred from the way of truth, and the light of justice hath not shined unto us, and the sun of understanding hath not risen upon us.
>
> We wearied ourselves in the way of iniquity and destruction, and have walked through hard ways, but the way of the Lord we have not known.
>
> What hath pride profited us? or what advantage hath the boasting of riches brought us?
>
> All those things are passed away like a shadow; and we have been consumed in our wickedness.[12]

Chapter II
We Have Our Sure Foundation upon God

MOREOVER, a rock is also in another respect an emblem of our Lord God, as the wisdom of God expounded in his Gospel when he said that a house built upon a rock would remain immovable, although the rain fell and the floods came and the winds blew; but a house built upon the sand cannot stand against any of these things, but as the first storm of rain, wind or floods it is cast down, and great shall be its fall.

Your abode, my soul, has different powers and faculties, as it were chambers or parlors. If it is built upon God as

---
[12] Wis. 5:6-9; 13.

upon a rock, i.e. if you firmly believe in God, if all your trust is in him, and your foundation is the love of God, so you could say with the Apostle, "Who shall separate us from the love of Christ?"[13] then be secure in the fact that neither the spiritual wickedness which assaults you from above, nor the carnal concupiscence from below, nor domestic enemies at your side, namely your friends and relations, will ever prevail against you by their temptations. Surely, the force and subtlety of spiritual powers is great, but greater still is the power and wisdom of the Holy Spirit, who rules in that house which is founded upon God. The flesh also fights eagerly against the spirit, and sometimes overcomes the strongest; but the love of God overcomes the love of the flesh, and the fear of God vanquishes the fear of the world. Even members of a man's household are his enemies,[14] and with their perverse counsels draw his soul into the company of sinners. But that soul which trusts that it has a Lord, a Father, a brother, and a spouse in heaven, will easily scorn and in that respect hate its carnal friends and relations, so as to say with the Apostle, "I am sure that neither death nor life, nor other creatures shall be able to separate us from the love of God which is in Christ Jesus our Lord."[15] Now, that soul is indeed miserable, whose house, since it was built upon sand, cannot stand for long; and the fall thereof will be great, because it belie lies, and trusts in a staff of reed, whose God is its belly, or money, or the smoke of honor. All such things pass away and perish very speedily and draw the soul which follows them into eternal ruin.

---

[13] Eph. 3:19.
[14] Mic. 7:6.
[15] Rom. 8:38-39.

CHAPTER III
The Earth Nourishes the Body by the Power of God, Who Alone Nourishes all Mankind

NOW, another property which has been placed in the earth is to plentifully bring forth herbs and fruit for the sustenance of men and animals, like a good nurse. This property directs us to our Maker, as to our true nursing Father, for not the earth, but God in the earth brings forth all good things. The Holy Spirit speaks this way through the mouth of David, "He that brings forth grass on the mountainsides, and an herb for the service of men,"[16] and again, "All wait upon you to give them food in due season. They will gather it as a gift from your hands; all will be filled with goodness from your open hand."[17] Our Lord also says in the Gospel: "Behold the birds of the air that neither sow nor reap, nor gather into barns, and your heavenly Father feeds them."[18] Then the Apostle, "and truly not without testimony has God left himself, bestowing benefits from heaven, giving rain and fruitful seasons, filling our hearts with food and joy."[19] Neither is that false which is said in the beginning of Genesis: "Let the earth bring forth green herbs and such as may seed, and fruit tree yielding fruits after its kind."[20] Although the earth brings forth herbs and fruit trees, yet it is by the virtue which God gave unto it, and God thereby keeps and increases. Thus, David, inviting all creatures to praise their maker, joins with the rest: "Fruitful

---

[16] Ps. 146 (147):8.
[17] Ps. 103 (104):27-28.
[18] Matt. 6:26.
[19] Act. 14:16.
[20] Gen. 1:2.

trees and all cedars,"[21] and the three children in Daniel are exhorted with all other things to bless the Lord, praise him, and exalt him above all forever.

Now, since all creatures after their manner praise God, with what emotion should you, O my soul, praise him for all of his benefits which you enjoy daily, acknowledging in them his fatherly love which never ceases to provide all things for you. Now, this is not much in the eyes of your Lord God, for he produces the noble branch of charity in you, as his spiritual field. Charity is not from the world, but from God,[22] as the most beloved disciple says in his Epistle. Charity also, as from a heavenly tree, brings forth the whitest flowers perfumed with holy thoughts, the greenest leaves of words aiding the salvation of nations, and the ripe fruits of good works whereby God is glorified, our neighbor edified, and its merits increased and preserved for eternal life.

Woe to those, however, who in the manner of stupid beasts long to be filled with the fruits of the earth, and gather and store them greedily, without giving a thought to their creator, nor give thanks for them. Their souls are like the earth which God cursed, so that it would bring forth thorns and thistles. What do they think, in whose minds God does not sow chaste intentions, but fornications, adultery, homicide, sacrilege, thefts, treacheries and the like? What do they speak but blasphemies, perjury, curses, heresies, abuse, contumelies, false testimonies, lies, and the like, which they learned from their father the devil? Lastly, what fruits do they bear but those whereof we have spoken, and which the Apostle calls "works of the flesh."[23] Truly these are the thorns which first prick the mind, which bring them forth, with bitter thoughts of fears and cares; and then

---

[21] Ps. 148:9.
[22] 1 Jn. 4:7.
[23] Gal. 5:19.

they prick the reputation, minds, and bodies of others with very serious, and often incurable wounds, whereby later many very serious harms come to others.

Now, passing over all of these, O my soul, if you will be a little garden of the heavenly farmer, beware lest thorns and thistles would ever be found in you; but with all care, cherish the tree of charity, the lily of chastity, and the spikenard of humility. Beware lest it ever enters into your mind to think that these branches of heavenly virtues come from yourself, and not from your Lord God, who is the Lord of virtues, the sower of chaste counsel, and do not attribute to yourself the preservation, increase, and ripeness of the fruit of good works, but as much as you can, commend them to God.

Chapter IV
The Treasures of the Earth Are, As It Were, A Shadowing of the Eternal Good Things of God.

THERE remains the last praise of the earth, that in her bosom gold, silver and precious stones are contained. Truly, the earth does not bring forth such precious kinds of things by her own power, but he who says through the prophet Haggai, "The silver is mine, and the gold is mine."[24] O lover of men, did it please your goodness, not only to produce stones, wood, iron, brass, lead, and similar things necessary for the building of houses, ships, and other instruments; but also gold, silver, and precious stones for beauty and decoration? Now, if you give these things to pilgrims on earth, and often also to your enemies who blaspheme your name, will you give to your friends who shall praise you and

---

[24] Hag. 2:9.

reign with you in heaven? You will give them, doubtless, not some little pieces of gold and silver, or some few precious stones, but that city of which John the Apostle speaks about in the Apocalypse, "And the building of the wall thereof was of jasper stone; but the city itself pure gold, and the foundations of the wall of the city were adorned with all manner of precious stones ... and the twelve gates are twelve pearls."[25]

But we must not imagine that heavenly city of Jerusalem is built or adorned with gold, pearls, and precious stones as they exist in this world. The Holy Spirit uses these words because he speaks to us who see no better or greater things. Yet, without a doubt that city, which is the country of God's elect, excels the cities of this pilgrimage far more than a city of gold and precious stones surpasses all country villages made of straw and clay.

So, O my soul, lift up the eyes of your mind to heaven, and consider how valuable are the riches there. Gold, silver, and precious stones which are so valuable in this world, are but straw and clay in comparison with the riches of heaven. The gold, silver, and precious stones which we have are also corruptible, but those which shine in that heavenly city are incorruptible. Now, if you will send your corruptible gold and silver by the hands of the poor into that heavenly city (which surely, if you are wise you will do), then it will become incorruptible and yours forever. For the truth cannot lie, who said, "Sell what you have and give to the poor, and you will have treasure in heaven,"[26] and again, "Sell what you possess and give alms. Make purses for yourself which do not grow old, a treasure in heaven which does not fail; where no thief comes near, nor moth corrupts."[27] O, the unbelief of the sons of men! Man, who is

---

[25] Apoc. 21:18-19; 21.
[26] Matt. 19:21.
[27] Lk. 12:33.

a liar, promises ten for a hundred, and to repay the whole lot to his lender, and he is believed. Now, God who cannot lie, promises a treasure in heaven to the man who gives alms, nay more, even a hundred for one, and that he will give eternal life; but the greedy man trembles and cannot easily be persuaded to believe, rather, he would hide his treasure where rust consumes it and thieves break in and steal, than lay it up in heaven, where there is neither rust to consume it nor thief to steal it.[28]

O unhappy man, even if it may happen that thieves do steal, or moth and rust corrupt that which you have gotten with labor and kept with care, nevertheless, it will not be yours as it might have been, if you had sent it into the heavenly treasury through the hands of the poor. Experience teaches us that the wealth which greedy rich men have gathered reaches prodigal heirs who waste it in a much shorter time than their greedy parents got it, whose sin of avarice will remain forever, where the worm of conscience does not die, and the fire of hell is not extinguished.[29]

Consequently, O my soul, let the foolishness of others teach you wisdom. Hear your Lord and master preaching: "See and beware of all avarice, for a man's life does not consist in the abundance of things which he possesses."[30] The greedy man gathers and preserves goods so that he may live for a long time, but it happens otherwise; when he is not thinking about it, he dies, and the wealth which he greedily gathered begets the worm that does not die, and lights the fire that will not be quenched. O, unhappy greedy man, why were you so anxious to gather together the money to prepare fuel for the fire of hell, which will never be extinguished? Listen to St. James in his last epistle, "Well

---

[28] Matt. 19:21.
[29] Mk. 9:47; Isa. 66:24.
[30] Lk. 12:15.

now, O rich men, weep and mourn in your miseries, which shall come upon you. Your riches are corrupted, and your garments have been eaten by moths. Your gold and silver have gone to rust, and the rust of them will bear testimony against you, and you will eat your flesh as fire."[31] You, St. James says, because you are rich, are considered to be happy, but indeed, you are more miserable than the poor. And you have great cause to lament, since the great miseries which assuredly shall fall upon you. The superfluous wealth you have kept and suffered to corrupt, when you ought to have given it to the poor; the superfluous garments that you possessed, and would rather let the moths eat than the poor be clothed with them; and your gold and silver, that which you would have to rust rather than bestow it to feed them; all these things, I say, will bear witness against you at the day of judgement, and the moths and rust of your wealth will be turned into a burning fire which will devour your flesh forever and not consume it, that the fire may not be quenched nor the pain ended. Let us, therefore, conclude with the kingly prophet: "They have said," namely the fools, "that the people which has these things is happy, but the happy people is the one whose God is the Lord."[32]

---

[31] Jas. 5:1-3.
[32] Ps. 143 (144):15.

THE FOURTH STEP
From the Consideration of the Waters and Especially of Founts

CHAPTER I
Water Washes the Stains of the Body; God Washes the Stains of the Soul

ATER has the second place among the elements of the world, and from rightly considering it, we may also frame a step of ascension unto God. First we will consider waters in general, and then we will draw a special ascension unto God from founts. Water is cold and moist, and has, as it were, five properties: it washes away stains, it quenches fire, it cools heat, it joins different things together, and, at length, as deeply as it goes down, it ascends as high. These things are manifest symbols, or vestiges of God the Creator of all. Water washes corporal stains, God washes spiritual stains. "You will wash me," David says, "And I will be whiter than snow."[1] Although contrition, the sacraments, priests, alms, and other works of piety wash away the stains, that is, the sins of the soul, still, they are but instruments or dispositions; the Author of this washing is God alone. Through Isaiah, God says, "I am, I am he that blots out your iniquities for my own sake."[2] Thus the Pharisees, when they murmured against Christ, said, "Who can forgive sins but

---

[1] Ps. 50(51):9.
[2] Isa. 43:25.

God alone?"[3] were not deceived in giving to God alone the supreme power to forgive sins, but because they did not believe that Christ was God, they both blasphemed and spoke the truth at the same time.

God does not only wash the stains of the soul like water. St. John writes: "He that believes in me, as Scripture says, out of his belly shall flow rivers of living water. Now this he said of the Spirit which they should receive, who believed in him; for as yet the Spirit was not given, because Jesus was not yet glorified."[4] Thus, God the Holy Spirit is living water, and Ezechiel speaks of him: "I will pour upon you clean water, and you shall be cleansed from all your filthiness."[5] Now, because this uncreated water far excels created water, we will set down three differences between the washing of the one and the other.

Created water washes away corporeal stains, but not all, for it cannot wash away many except by soap or other instruments. Uncreated water altogether washes stains, just as we read again in Ezechiel, "You shall be cleansed from all of your filthiness."

Created water rarely washes all stains in such a way that some vestige, or shadow of the stain is not left. Uncreated water washes to such an extent that the thing washed is rendered more glorious and beautiful than it was polluted, as David says, "You will wash me, and I will be whiter than snow,"[6] and our Lord says through Isaiah, "If your sins be as scarlet, they shall be made as white as snow; and if they are as red as crimson, they will be as white as wool."[7]

Next, created water washes natural stains, which do not resist cleansing; uncreated water washes voluntary stains,

---

[3] Lk. 5:21.
[4] Jn. 7:38-39.
[5] Ez. 36:25.
[6] Ps. 50 (51):9.
[7] Isa. 1:18.

which cannot be washed unless the soul itself were to will it, and consent to them being washed away of its own will. So admirable is the power of this water, that it sweetly enters into hardened hearts and is not refused, because, as St. Augustine rightly teaches.[8] Who can grasp, O Lord, how you give faith to the unfaithful, humility to the proud, and charity to your enemies, that he who once breathed forth threats and slaughter, and persecuted you in your disciples, being changed all of the sudden, so willingly suffered threats and persecutions for you and your Church?[9] Far be it for me to dive into your secrets, for I would rather experience than search after the efficacy of your grace. Now, because I know that water of yours is a willing rain, separated to your inheritance,[10] as the prophet sings; therefore, I humbly beg you, let me be found in your inheritance, and may it please your grace to descend into the earth of my heart, so that it would not remain like the earth without water from you, arid and sterile, the kind that of itself does not even suffice to conceive of anything good. Now, let us continue to the rest.

Chapter II
Water Extinguishes Fire; God Quenches the Flames of Lust

WATER extinguishes fire; and that heavenly water, namely the grace of the Holy Spirit extinguishes the fire of carnal lust in a wonderful manner. It is true enough that fasting and bodily afflictions are a powerful means to quench this fiery passion if they are applied as instruments of grace, otherwise, of themselves they do not avail much. Love is the

---

[8] *De Praedest. SS.* C. 8 n. 13.
[9] Act. 9:1, *seqq.*.
[10] Ps. 57 (58):10.

chief among the affections and disturbances of the mind, which rules all and is obeyed by all. Love will not be compelled, and it is stopped one way, it breaks out in another. Love fears nothing, dares everything, and conquers all; it reckons nothing difficult or impossible for it, and at length, a lesser love yields to nothing except a greater and stronger love. So, an altogether carnal love pursues the wealth and pleasures of the world, yields only to the love of God; at the very moment in which the water of the Holy Spirit begins to pour into the heart of man, right away carnal love begins to cool. St. Augustine is a witness to this, who, being long accustomed to lust, thought it impossible to lack the company of a woman; yet beginning to taste the grace of the Holy Spirit, he cried out in the *Confessions*, "How sweet it was to me all of the sudden, to be without trifling pleasures, and what before I feared to lose, I now rejoiced to forsake. For you, the true and ultimate happiness, cast them from me; you cast them from me, and entered in their stead more sweet than any pleasure, but not to flesh and blood; more bright than any light, more inward than any secret; loftier than any honor, but not to those who are lofty in themselves."[11]

Chapter III
Water Quenches Thirst; God Quenches the Desires of the Heart

WATER also quenches thirst, but only the water of the Holy Spirit can quench the manifold and almost endless desires of man's heart. Truth plainly taught this, when it spoke to the Samaritan woman, "Everyone that drinks of this water shall

---

[11] *Confess.* 9, 1.

thirst again; but he that shall drink of the water that I will give him, he shall not thirst forever."[12] Indeed, so it is, "The eye is not filled with seeing, nor is the ear filled with hearing."[13] For the mind of man is capable of infinite good, and all creatures are finite. Yet, once a man begins to drink of this divine water, in which all things are, he neither desires nor requires anything further. And we spoke of this before, when we said that the our souls have their rest in God alone, as in their proper center.

Chapter IV
Water Joins Corporeal Things Together; God Achieves the Union of Spiritual Things

WATER joins different things together as many grains of flour are joined with water through a mixture to make one loaf, and bricks are made from many parts of earth by a mixture of water. Now, the water of the Holy Spirit causes many men to be of one heart and one soul more easily and inseparably, as we read in the Acts of the Apostles of the first Christians, upon whom the Holy Spirit descended after the Apostles. And the Lord, being about to ascend to his Father, commends that unity which the water of the Holy Spirit causes, saying, "And not for them alone do I pray, but for them also who through their word shall believe in me; that they all may be one, as you father, in me and I in you, that they also may be one in us. ... That they may be one as we also are one. I in them and you in me, that they me be completed in one." The Apostle also exhorts us to such a unity when he says, "Be careful to keep the unity of the

---

[12] Jn. 4:13.
[13] Eccl. 1:8.

Spirit in the bond of peace. One body and one Spirit; as you are called in one hope of your calling."[14] O happy union which makes many men one body of Christ, governed by one head, partaking of one bread, drinking of one cup, and living by one spirit of God, is made one spirit with him. What can his servants desire more than to partake not only of all their master's goods, but also by the inseparable bond of love to be made one with the Almighty? All which is wrought by the grace of the Holy Spirit, when, as living water, it is devoutly received and diligently kept in the heart.

CHAPTER V
Water Descends and Ascends Again; the Fount of God's Grace Gushes Forth unto Eternal Life

LASTLY, water ascends as high as it descends low. And as the Holy Spirit came from heaven to earth, so that heart in which he is received is made a "fountain of water springing up unto everlasting life,"[15] as our Lord said to the Samaritan woman. This means that a man born again of water and the Holy Spirit, who has the same Spirit dwelling within him, causes his merits to ascend from where grace descended.

So, O my soul, being instructed and encouraged by these passages of Scripture, say to your heavenly Father as often as you can with sighs beyond description: Give me this water which washes all stains clean, quenches all fire of lust, cools all heat of thirst, and makes me one spirit with my God, that being in me a fountain of water springing up into life everlasting, it may cause in me merits to ascend there,

---

[14] Eph. 4:3-4.
[15] Jn. 4:14.

The Fourth Step: A Consideration of Water

where I hope to live forever. It is not without reason that the Son of God said, "If when you are evil, you know to give good things to your sons, how much more will your Father in heaven give a good spirit to those that ask him?"[16] And he does not say that he will give bread, clothes, wisdom, charity, or everlasting life, rather, "the good Spirit," for all things are contained in it. Do not cease, O my soul, to admonish the Father of the promise of his Son, saying with great devotion and assured hope to obtain: O holy Father, not in my own justification do I pray to you, but in the promise of your only begotten Son. For he has said unto us, "How much more will your Father in heaven give the good Spirit to those that ask him?" Surely your Son is the Truth,[17] he does not deceive us; so fulfill the promise of your Son who has glorified you upon the earth,[18] and was obedient to you unto death, even the death of the Cross.[19] Give the "good Spirit" to those who ask it of you. Give the spirit of your love and fear, so that your servant would love nothing but you, and his neighbor in You, nor fear anything except offending You: "Create a clean heart in me, O God: and renew a right spirit in my bowels. Cast me not away from your face, and your Holy Spirit do not take from me. Render me the joy of your salvation, and confirm me with a principal spirit."[20]

---

[16] Lk. 11:13.
[17] John 14:6.
[18] John 17:4.
[19] Phil. 2:8.
[20] Ps. 50 (51): 12-14.

Chapter VI
A Fount of Water Is the Image of God as the Fount of our Being

I COME now to the similitude which founts of water have with God, for from them the mind may also be lifted to consider his wonderful works. Now, it is not without cause that in Holy Scripture, God is called "a fount of eternal life and wisdom,"[21] and a "fount of living water."[22] That he is the Fount of being, we gather from these words which God spoke to Moses, "I am who am; he who is hath sent me to you."[23] All which the Apostle seems to have included when he says, "In him we live and move and be."[24] In him we are, as in a fount of being; in him we live, as in a fount of life; and in him we move, a in a fount of wisdom; because "Wisdom is more active than all active things; and reaches everywhere by reason of her purity."[25]

A fount of water among us has this property, that rivers spring from it, and when they cease to flow from their fount they are soon dried up; but the fount depends not upon the rivers, because it does not receive water from them, rather, form itself, and it gives it to others. This is a true resemblance of the divinity; for God is the truest Fount of being; because he receives his being from no other thing; but all things received their being from him. God received his being from no other thing, because his essence is to exist, and his being is his existence; so that it cannot be conceived or come to pass that God has not always existed and always will exist. Other things may exist for a time, and for a time

---

[21] Ps. 35 (36):10; Eccl. 1:5.
[22] Jer. 2:13.
[23] Exod. 3:14.
[24] Act. 17:28.
[25] Wis. 7:24.

The Fourth Step: A Consideration of Water

then not exist, because existence does not belong by necessity to their essence. For example, it belongs to the essence of a man to be a rational creature; and therefore, he cannot be a man unless he is a rational creature; and if existence also belongs to the essence of a man, he should then always exist; but because it belongs not to his essence, as a result, he may exist and not exist. God, then, is the Fount of being, because his essence includes actual existence forever, as is signified by those words, "I am who am."[26] That is, I am essence itself, and do not receive My being from any other thing, for to Me alone My essence is My existence. As a result, eternity and immortality is proper to God alone, as the Apostle declares, "To the immortal king of ages, God alone,"[27] and who alone has immortality.[28] All other things receive their being from God, that unless they always depend upon him, and are preserved by him, they presently cease to exist. This is why the same Apostle says, "Who carries all things by the word of his power."[29]

So, my soul, admire and reverence the infinite goodness of your Maker, who maintains or preserves all things so lovingly, although he does not need their service. Admire and imitate also, the patience of your Creator, who is so "merciful upon the unkind and the evil,"[30] that he feeds and preserves those who blaspheme him, and deserve to be brought to nothing. So, let it not seem much unto you to bear for a while with the infirmities of your brethren, and as you are bidden to do good to those who hate you.

Now, the existence of a fount does not merely consist in not receiving being from another fount, and in giving being to other things; for the water both of founts and rivers with

---

[26] Exod. 3:14.
[27] 1 Tim. 1:17.
[28] 1 Tim. 6:17.
[29] Heb. 1:3.
[30] Lk. 6:35.

us is the same kind and albeit that founts do not receive their water from other founts, yet they have a cause of their being, namely vapors, which also have other successive causes, until we come unto God, the first cause. Still, God your Maker, O my soul, is not of the same kind with creatures, but infinitely surpasses them in dignity, nobility, and excellence. He is also truly and properly the Fount of being, not only because he did not receive his being from another fount of being, but also for that he has no cause at all. A fount of created water, as is said, is not derived from any other water, but from another cause; yet the uncreated Fount of being has nothing before himself, depends upon nothing, wants nothing, and is harmed by nothing; rather all things depend upon him, and he can destroy all creation with but a nod.[31]

Now, admire this excellence, O my soul, this beginning without beginning, this cause without cause, this essence that is infinite, unlimited, immense, and absolutely necessary in comparison to which all other things are merely contingent. Perhaps Truth spoke of himself when he said, "But one thing is necessary."[32] Hence, adhere to him alone, serve him alone, and delight in his love alone. Despise all other things for his sake, or else do not be troubled with too much anxiety about so many things, since one thing is necessary, which alone is enough for you and all others. Instead, be careful never to fall from his grace, studying always and everywhere how to please him.

---

[31] 2 Macc. 8:18.
[32] Lk. 10:42.

CHAPTER VII
God Dwelling in Himself Is the Fount of Life

GOD is also most truly called a Fount of life, because he "has life in himself,"[33] and is eternal life itself: "He is the true God and eternal life," says John.[34] All things that live receive life from that fount, which when it shall cease to give them life, "they shall fall and return to their dust,"[35] as the holy prophet David says. It is proper for living creatures to beget like unto themselves. God also begot a Son most like to himself, "For as the Father has life in himself, so he has given also to the Son to have life in himself,"[36] as St. John witnesses in the Gospel; but the Father has life in himself, because he is the fount of life, and does not receive life otherwise; and the Son has life in himself, because the Father has given him the same life which he has, whereby the Son also is the fount of life, but the fount of life of the fount of life, as God of God, and light of light. Who can declare or even conceive what the life of God is, and what this fount of life is, from where all things that live in heaven or on earth draw drops of life? The life which we have known in this banishment is none other than the internal beginning of motion; for those things we say live which move themselves after some manner. Consequently, the water of rivers is commonly called running or living water, because it seems to move of itself, and the water of ponds, standing or dead water, for that is not moved but by the winds of some other external force.

Your God, O my soul, most ruly lives and is the author

---

[33] Jn. 5:26.
[34] 1 Jn. 5:20.
[35] Ps. 103 (104):29.
[36] John 5:26.

and fount of life. Often in Holy Scripture, he drives this point home, saying, "Live, I, says our Lord,"[37] and the prophets often repeat: "The Lord lives, the Lord lives," and in Jeremiah God complains of the people, saying: "They have forsaken me, the fount of living water."[38] Yet, he is not moved either by himself or by any other; "I am God" he says, "and am not changed."[39] And again, "God is not as the son of man that he may be changed."[40] We sing also in the ecclesiastical hymn:

> *Rerum Deus tenans vigor*
> *Immotus in te permanens,*
> *Lucis diurna tempora*
> *Successibus determinans.*[41]

Even if God begets a Son, he begets him without change. And if he sees, hears, speaks, loves, pardons, or judges, he does them all without change; and if he creates and preserves, or destroys and dissipates, and again renews and changes, he yet works all this while at rest and changes without being changed. How then does he live, if he does not move? And how does he not live if he is the fount and author of life? This knot is easily untied. To live it is absolutely enough that the thing which lives works of itself, and is not moved by another; but life for the most part in created things is the internal beginning of motion, because created things are imperfect, and need many things to perform the actions of life; but God is infinite perfection, and

---

[37] Num. 24:28.
[38] Jer. 2:3.
[39] Mal. 3:6.
[40] Num. 32:19.
[41] O God, whose power unmoved the whole
Of Nature's vastness doth control,
Who mark'st the day-hours as they run
By steady marches of the sun.

needs nothing outside of himself, and, therefore, he works of himself and is not moved by any other.

Creatures need change to beget and be begotten, because they beget outside themselves, and the thing begotten must be changed from non being to being. God, however, begot a Son within himself, and within himself produces the Holy Spirit. Neither should the Son nor the Holy Spirit be changed from non being to being, because they receive that being which always was, and they do not receive it in time but eternity.

Created things need the motion of increase, because they are born imperfect, but God the Son is born most perfect, and God the Holy Spirit is breathed and produced most perfect. Created things need the motion of alteration to attain different qualities which they want; but God wants nothing, since his essence is of infinite perfection. Created things need local motion, because they are not everywhere; but God is wholly everywhere. Moreover, creatures need many things to see, hear, speak, and work, because their life is poor and imperfect; but God does not need anything outside of himself to see all, hear all, speak to all, and work all; not only does he have life, but the richest and happiest life, and he is life itself, as well as the fount of life. Now, let us place an example in the action of sight. For a man to see, he needs the power to do so, which is distinct from the soul which properly sees; he needs an object, that is, a colored body outside of himself; he needs the light of the sun, or of some other luminous body. He needs a medium, that is a clear body; he needs a sensible species or form, to be carried from the object to the eye; he needs a corporeal organ, namely an eye endowed with humors and fleshy muscles; he needs sensitive spirits and optic sinews, whereby those spirits must pass; he needs a proportionate distance and lastly, he needs the application of the seeing power, or faculty. Behold how many things men and other living creatures want to perform one action of life; but God, who truly has all life in himself, needs nothing. His infinite essence includes power, form, object, light and all other things. God, of himself, by himself, and in himself, sees all things, which are, have been, or shall be, and evidently knows all things which may be. Now, before the world was made, God saw all things, so that by the creation of things there came nothing but was before known unto him.

What will you be then, O my soul, when you partake of that life? Is it much that God commands you, when he would have you spend this corporeal, animal, needy and imperfect life for himself and your brethren to obtain eternal life? Now, if he does not command much, when he commands this life to be condemned, how light and trifling should it seem to you, when he commands you to bestow your dead riches upon the poor; and to refrain from carnal concupiscence, to renounce the devil and his allurements, and with true devotion of heart to sigh after that life which alone is true life.

Chapter VIII
God the Fount of Wisdom

NOW it is time to ascend, in whatever way we can, to the fount of wisdom. "The word of God on high is the fount of wisdom,"[42] says Sirach, and rightly he says "on high", because the Fount of wisdom plentifully flows upon the holy angels and blessed souls in heaven. Yet unto us who inhabit this desert and pilgrimage, wisdom herself does not descend, but a certain hint or vapor of wisdom.

This is why, O my soul, seek not after higher things than

---

[42] Sirach 1:5.

are fitting for you, "A man that searches out the majesty will be oppressed by glory."[43] Admire his wisdom, of which the Apostle speaks, "To God the only wise."[44] Congratulate those blessed spirits which drink of the fount of wisdom; and although they do not fully grasp God, which is only proper to the very fount itself, yet they behold the face of God, which is the first cause, without veil, beaming with his brightness, they truly judge all things, not fearing in that noonday light of wisdom the darkness of error, the blindness of ignorance, or the fog of opinions. Seek after that happiness, and that you may surely attain to it, love our Lord Jesus Christ with all of your heart, "In whom are all the treasures of wisdom and knowledge of God."[45] He said in the Gospel, "He that loves me will be beloved of my Father, and I will love him and will manifest myself to him."[46] Now, what does it mean, "I will manifest myself to him," except that I will manifest to him the treasures of wisdom and knowledge which are in me? Truly, every man naturally desires knowledge, and although carnal concupiscence now dull this desire in many by a certain measure, nevertheless, when this corruptible body will be laid aside, which now dulls the soul, then will the fire of this desire break forth more than any other.

How great will your happiness be then, my soul, when your love and beloved, Christ, will show you "the treasures of the wisdom and knowledge of God?" Lest you be frustrated of so great a hope, endeavor to keep the commandments of Christ; for he said, "If anyone love me, he will keep my word; and he that loves me not, does not keep my words,"[47] and in the meantime, hold onto that wisdom

---

[43] Prov. 25:27.
[44] Rom. 16:27.
[45] Col. 2:3.
[46] Jn. 14:21.
[47] Jn. 14:23-24.

which holy Job describes, saying, "The fear of God, that is wisdom, and to depart from evil, understanding."[48] Whatever goodness you see in created things, acknowledge it to be derived from God, the fount of all goodness, that here in the rivers of creatures you may begin to taste of that fount, as St. Francis did.[49]

---

[48] Job 28:28.
[49] St. Bonaventure, *Life of St. Francis*, c. 9.

THE FIFTH STEP
From the Consideration of the Air

CHAPTER I
The Body Lives by Air, the Soul by Prayer

HE element of air can be a notable teacher of morals to men, if its nature were considered. Not only is it best suited to teach men moral philosophy, but also to open to them the mysteries of sacred Theology, and to elevate the mind to God, if anyone would wish to attend to the various advantages, which the air continually furnishes to the human race by God's ordinance.

In the first place, the air serves for breathing, and thereby preserves the life of man and of terrestrial living creatures. Next, it is so necessary for sight, hearing, and speech that without it, though nothing else were absent, no one could see, hear, or speak. Lastly, without the air, there could be no motion among men and other terrestrial living creatures, so that all arts and sciences would need to come to an end. Let us begin with the first part.

If men were to understand that the soul needs her breathing as much as the body, many men who now perish would be saved. The soul needs continual respiration, because the natural heat whereby the heart boils, is so tempered by the lungs which draw in the cool air and cast out the hot, that life is thereby preserved, without which it could not exist; whereupon, it is commonly said that those things which breathe are alive, and those things which do not breathe are dead. Now you, O my soul, to live a spiritual life by God's grace, you will also want your continual breathing, which is performed by sending forth warm sighs in your prayers to God, and receiving from God the new grace of the Holy Spirit. What else does Our Lord mean when he says, "We must pray always, and not to falter,"[1] except that you might always sigh and receive a new spirit, that the spiritual life would not be extinguished in you? He repeats this when he says, "Watch, praying at all times."[2] The Apostle also confirms the same thing when he says, "Pray without ceasing."[3] St. Peter the Apostle is in full agreement, when he writes, "Be prudent therefore, and watch in prayer."[4] For true wisdom wills us to ask God's help at all times, which we are always in need of. Our heavenly Father truly knows what we want, and is prepared to give abundantly unto us, especially if it belongs to our eternal salvation; but he will give it to us by means of prayer, for that is more to his honor and our benefit, than if he were to give us all things when we sleep and do nothing.

Consequently, our most generous Lord exhorts and urges us to ask when he says, "Ask and it shall be given you seek and you shall find; knock, and it shall be opened to you."[5] And what is chiefly to be asked, and what without doubt shall be granted, he declares a little after saying, "If you, being evil, know how to give good gifts to your children, how much more will your Father from heaven give the good Spirit to anyone who asks him?"[6] Therefore, we principally must ask for this good Spirit daily, which without a doubt will be given to us if we ask well, whereby we may breathe in God, and by breathing him in preserve

---

[1] Lk. 18:1.
[2] Luke 21:36.
[3] 1 Thess. 5:17.
[4] 1 Pet. 4:7.
[5] Lk. 9:9.
[6] Lk. 11:13.

The Fifth Step: A Consideration of the Air

our spiritual life. This is what David did, who says in the Psalm, "I opened my mouth, and drew breath,"[7] i.e. I opened my mouth, desiring, sighing, craving with inexplicable sighs, and I drew the sweetest breath of God's Spirit, which cooled the heat of my concupiscence, and strengthened me in every good work. Since this is so, who can say that they live for God, who through whole days, months, and years, do not sigh after him nor breathe him in? Not breathing is a clear sign of death. The spiritual life, in which we become sons of God, consists in charity, as St. John says, "Behold what manner of charity the Father has bestowed upon us, that we should be called, and really should be the sons of God."[8] And who is there that loves, but desires to see the thing he loves? Who desires anything and doesn't ask for it, when he knows that by asking for it he will receive it? As a result, the man who does not daily pray to see the face of his God, does not desire to see him; if he does not desire to see him, he doesn't love him; if he does not love him, he does not live. What follows then except that we count them as dead to God, although they live for the world, because they do not give themselves to prayer? Moreover, men such as these are not understood to pray, and thereby to breathe and live, when they merely pray with their corporeal voice. Prayer is defined by the learned not as lifting of the voice into the air, *but as an elevation of the mind to God.*

Thus, O my soul, do not deceive yourself, thinking that you live for God unless you seek God with all of your heart, and sigh after him day and night. Do not say that you are too busy to give yourself to prayer and spiritual exercises, since the Holy Apostles were very busy, albeit it was in the work of God and salvation of souls, so that one of them said, "Besides those things which are on the outside, my daily burdens, the solicitude for all the Churches. Who is weak,

---

[7] Ps. 118:131.
[8] 1 Jn. 3:1.

and I am not weak? Who is scandalized, and I am not on fire?"[9] Yet, the same Apostle, apart from the frequent commemoration of his prayers,[10] writes, "Our conversation is in heaven."[11] In the midst of business, in desire he was in heaven, or else he would not have said, "I am nailed to the cross with Christ, but I live, now not I, but Christ lives in me."[12]

Chapter II
The Air Considered as the Medium of Living, Hearing, and Speaking.

ANOTHER property of the air is that it becomes the medium whereby the spectrum of colors come to our eyes, and the range of sounds to our ears, without which we could neither see, nor hear, nor even speak. This is why we should give great thanks to God that it has pleased him to beautify our nature with so singular a benefit. We should also admire the wisdom of our maker in a work of such great subtlety; for although the air is a true body and so great that it fills a nearly infinite space, yet it is neither seen nor felt, by reason of its incredible thinness. Antiquity marveled at the thinness of a line which Appelles had drawn with a pencil; but that line was seen and touched, and, as a result, not to be compared with the thinness of the air, which covers and embraces all things, and yet is seen by none. It is also the more to be marveled at that the air, which is so thin a body, is still divided and closes again together with such ease, and remains as though it had never been divided. Truly, it is not

---

[9] 2 Cor. 11:28-29.
[10] Rom. 1:10; 1 Thess. 1:2; 2 Tim. 1:3.
[11] Phil. 3:20.
[12] Gat.. 2:19-20.

The Fifth Step: A Consideration of the Air   63

possible for a craftsman to amend a spider's broken web, or a tear in a very thin veil in such a way that the tear will not still appear. It is also most worthy of admiration and only belongs to the wisdom of God, to cause innumerable types of colors to pass together without confusion through the same part of the air. A man who stands in a high and open place in the evening when the moon shines, and he beholds the heaven full of stars and fields full of flowers, with houses, trees, animals, and other things of this sort, he cannot deny but that the species or forms of those things are contained in the air next to him altogether without confusion. Who can conceive this? How can it be that so thin a body contains together such a variety of forms? And what if, at the same time and place, birds sing, musical instruments play, and waters falling make a noise; are those sounds or forms of sounds not received altogether with so many colors or forms of colors in the same air? Who performs these things, O my soul, except your Maker, "who alone does great wonders?"[13] If his works are so wonderful, how much more wonderful is he himself?

Now, another useful property of this admirable thinness in the air is that it does not impede motion, rather, it helps them move from place to place. We all know how much work it is to tow ships through the waters, even though they are liquid and easily divided. Sometimes neither winds nor oars are enough, rather, the strength of horses and oxen must be added. Now, if perhaps a road were to be made through the hills and mountains, no matter how short it is, what sweat would be required take to make it, and how long it would take! Yet, horses run in the air, birds fly, and arrows and bullets are shot with great ease and speed; men also go up and down about their business and move their feet, arms, and hands, up, down, from left to right, and yet the air.

---

[13] Ps. 135 (136):4.

Although it is diffused everywhere the air does not impede them as if it were not of a corporeal, but a spiritual nature, or nothing at all.

Chapter III
We Observe in the Air, as it Were, a Type of the Sweetness and Mercy of God

LASTLY, it is the nature of air to yield to everything, to change itself into every form, and to allow itself to be torn and broken so that it would serve the needs of man, so that it would seem to have been given to men as a teacher of humility, patience, and charity. It likewise represents to men the incredible sweetness and exceeding bounty of the Maker thereof. Think of yourself, O my soul, and consider very attentively that your Lord God is always present with his creatures, always works with them, and, from his infinite sweetness accommodates himself to everyone's character. It is as if he were to say with the Apostle, "I became all things to all men,"[14] that I might help and perfect all; he works with necessary agents so that they would do what is necessary; with willing agents that they might act willingly, with free agents so they would act freely. He moves and helps fire to go up, the earth to go down, the water to fall into deep places, the air to pass whichever way it is pushed; the stars to turn in a perpetual circle; grass, shrubs and seedlings to bear fruit according to their nature; animals of the earth, fishes, and birds to do what their nature requires. Now, if the sweetness of God appears so clearly in cooperation with his creatures in the works of nature, what ought we to think of the works of grace?

---

[14] 1 Cor. 9:22.

The Fifth Step: A Consideration of the Air

Truly God has given man free will, yet so that it is ruled by his commandments, terrified by his punishments, and allured by his benefits. God wills all men to be saved,[15] but he wills it in such a way that he wills them to will also, and therefore, he sweetly prevents, excites, leads, and directs them in such a way, that it is wonderful to consider. These are the inventions of the wisdom of God, on which Isaiah speaks: "Make known his inventions among the people."[16] Sometimes he forcefully terrifies wicked men, sometimes he lovingly exhorts them, sometimes he mercifully admonishes them, as he thinks is most expedient to their natures and conditions. Hear how mercifully God dealt with Adam, the first sinner: "The Lord God called Adam and said, 'Where are you?' And he said, 'I heard your voice in paradise; and I was afraid, because I was naked, and hid myself.'" God mercifully replied, "Who told you that you were naked, except that you have eaten of the tree which I commanded you not to eat?"[17] And Adam, being admonished by this pious correction, did repent, for Scripture says, "She [i.e. the wisdom of God] preserved him who was first formed by God the Father of the world, ... and she brought him out of his sin."[18] Let us listen again to how mercifully God corrected the children of Israel by his angel, and provoked them to repentance, "The angel of the Lord went up from Galgal to the place of weepers, and said: I made you go out of Egypt, and have brought you into the land which I swore to your fathers, and I promised that I would not make void my covenant with you forever, so that you would not make a league with the inhabitants of this land, rather, would throw down their altars, and you would not hear my voice; why have you done this? And when the angel of the Lord spoke

---

[15] 1 Tim. 2:4.
[16] Isa. 12:49.
[17] Gen. 3:9-11.
[18] Wis. 10:1-2.

these words to all the children of Israel, they lifted up their voice and wept. And the name of that place was called, 'The place of weepers,' or 'of tears,' and there they offered sacrifices to the Lord."[19] Now, the new name given to that place bears the eternal witness to posterity that it was a great and general lamentation, and a sign of true repentance, since it was called "the place of weepers, or of tears." What shall I say of the prophets? They teach and proclaim in all of their preaching that, "God does not desire the death of sinners, rather, that they would be converted and live."[20] Jeremiah says, "It is commonly said: If a man put away his wife, and she goes from him and marries another man, shall he return to her any more? shall not that woman be polluted and defiled? but you have prostituted yourself to many lovers: nevertheless return to me, says the Lord, and I will receive you." And again by Ezechiel, "Thus you have spoken, saying: Our iniquities and our sins are upon us, and we pine away in them; how then can we live? Say to them: As I live, says the Lord God, I desire not the death of the wicked, but that the wicked would turn from their way and live. Turn then, turn from your evil ways, and why will you die, O house of Israel?"[21] Now, passing over the wicked, in no way can it be expressed how much more the kindness and sweetness of the Lord God is than fatherly or motherly goodness to those who hope and fear him. David in the Psalms says, "According to the height of heaven from the earth, has he strengthened his mercy upon those that fear him... As a Father has compassion on his children, so our Lord has compassion on those that fear him. ... The mercy of our Lord is from eternity and unto eternity upon those that fear him."[22] Then in another place, "Taste and see that our

---

[19] Judg. 2:1-2, 4-5.
[20] Ezech. 33:10-11.
[21] Ezech. 23:10-11.
[22] Ps. 102 (103):11, 13, 17.

Lord is sweet, blessed is the man that hopes in him."[23] Again, "How good is God to Israel and to those who are pure of heart,"[24] i.e. who can express the great goodness, mercy, and sweetness of God unto righteous souls? God also says by Isaiah, "Can a woman forget her child, that she will not have pity on the son of her womb? And if she would forget, yet I will not forget you."[25] Then, Jeremiah says in his Lamentations, "Our Lord is my portion, said my soul; therefore I will wait for him. Our Lord is good to those who hope in him, to the soul that seek him. It is good to wait with silence for the salvation of God."[26]

If I were to add what the Apostles say in their Epistles of the love of God towards the righteous, I would never come to an end. Let what St. Paul wrote stand for all, "Blessed be the God and Father of our Lord Jesus Christ, the Father of mercies, and the God of all comfort. Who comforts us in all our tribulation, so that we also may be able to comfort them who are in all distress."[27] He does not say that God is a comforter, but full "of all comfort;" not that he comforts us in some tribulation, but in "all tribulation;" not that we may be able to comfort those who are in distress, but in "all distress." Thus, a man could not enlarge any more upon how sweet God is towards those who love him, and by whom he is loved.

Now to bring this to an end, we will apply the words of St. Prosper of Aquitaine, wherein he declares the mercy of God not only to the righteous, but also to the wicked, so as to make them righteous, "Grace principally excels all justification by persuading with exhortations, by admonishing with examples, by terrifying with dangers, by

---

[23] Ps. 33 (34) :9.
[24] Ps. 72 (73):1.
[25] Isa. 49:15.
[26] Lam. 3:24-26.
[27] 2 Cor. 1:3-4.

arousing with miracles, by giving understanding, by inspiring counsel, by illuminating the heart and endowing it with dispositions of faith. Yet, even the human will is subdued and joined to it, which, as a result, is roused to it by the aforesaid aids, to cooperate with the divine work in itself, and begin to use for merit what it conceived from heavenly seed for zeal, proceeding from its own fickleness if it decays, and from the aid of grace if it takes effect. That is aid is given to all in countless ways, whether secret or manifest; and when many refuse it, it proceeds from their wickedness, but when many receive it, it is a work of divine grace and human will."[28]

Chapter IV
Exhortation of the Soul to the Imitation of the Kindness of God

How now my soul, if your maker is so sweet and merciful towards his servants and puts up with sinners with such incredible kindness so as to convert them, and comforting the righteous to increase their virtue all the more, should you not meekly put up with your neighbors, and "to become all things to all men so as to gain all unto your Lord God"?[29] Think within yourself to what a high excellence the Apostle calls you, when he says, "Be followers of God as most dear children, and walk in love as Christ has also loved us, and delivered himself for us, as an oblation to God for an odor of sweetness." Imitate God the Father, "who causes his sun to rise upon the good and the wicked, and rain to fall upon the just and the unjust."[30] Imitate God the Son, who, having taken human nature, did not spare his own life to deliver us

---
[28] *De Vocat. Gent.* 2, 26.
[29] 1 Cor. 9:19.
[30] Matt. 5:45.

from the power of darkness and eternal ruin. Imitate God the Holy Spirit, who plentifully pours out his most precious gifts unto us, to brings it about that we become spiritual beings from carnal.

THE SIXTH STEP
From a Consideration of Fire

CHAPTER I
The Hatred of God Against Sin Is as a Consuming Fire

HE ELEMENT of fire is so pure and noble that God himself willed to be called fire, as Moses and St. Paul say: "Our God is a consuming fire."[1] When God first appeared to Moses, he appeared in a fire burning a bush but not consuming it, "The Lord appeared to him in a flame of fire out of the midst of a bush; and he saw that the bush was on fire and was not burnt."[2] When the same God came to give the Law to the people, he came in the form of fire. "All of Mount Sinai smoked; for because our Lord was descended upon it in fire."[3] When the New Law was about to be promulgated, the Holy Spirit appeared in a likeness of this mystery. Next, those spirits which are nearest to God in heaven are called *seraphim*, which means fiery, because they are more inflamed with the fire of divine love than other angels. This being so, it is not difficult to set up a step on the ladder from the element of fire or its nature and properties, whereby through meditation and prayer we might ascend to God. Surely it will be easier to go up with Elijah in a fiery chariot than to make a ladder of earth, water, or air.

So, let us consider the properties of the fire! The fire is

---

[1] Deut. 4:24; Heb. 12:29.
[2] Exod. 3:2.
[3] Exod. 19:18.

of such a nature, that in different things often works in a different and often contrary matter. It immediately consumes wood, grass, stubble right away; gold, silver, and precious stones it renders more pure and beautiful. Iron, which by its own nature is black, cold, hard and heavy, fire so changes into contrary qualities, that presently it is rendered white, hot, soft, and light, nay more, it shines like a star, to burn like fire, to melt like water, and to be so light that a blacksmith may very easily move and lift it as he pleases. All these things clearly come together in God. First, wood, grass, and stubble, according to the Apostle, signify evil works, which cannot endure the fire of the divine judgment.[4] Indeed, it is incredible how vehemently sins displease God, who is the purest fire, and with what zeal he consumes and destroys them, if they can be destroyed by penance, i.e, if a man who sinned is in a state to be able to do penance, for all sins are loosed by penance. If, however, the sinner is not capable of penance, just as the demons and men after this life, then the divine wrath is turned against him, and as the wise man says, "For God the wicked and his wickedness are hateful alike."[5] Truly the devil can witness how great this hate is, since he once sinned and was a very noble angel, and as St. Gregory says, prince of the first order and the most excellent of God's creatures, nevertheless he was immediately cast down from heaven, deprived of all beauty, and supernatural grace, changed into a most deformed monster, and condemned to eternal ruin.[6] Christ is a witness, who descended from heaven to destroy the works of the devil, namely sins, and so is called the "Lamb of God that takes away the sins of the world."[7] Now, who can conceive or explain what Christ suffered to destroy the

---

[4] 1 Cor. 3:12-13.
[5] Wis. 14:9.
[6] *Moral.* 33:24.
[7] John 1:29.

The Sixth Step: A Consideration of Fire

works of the devil[8] and perfectly satisfy the justice of God? Who "although he was in the form of God, took the form of a servant,[9] being made poor for us when he was rich."[10] He had no place to lay his head,[11] albeit he made heaven and earth. "He came unto his own, and his own did not receive him.[12] Who, when he was cursed, did not curse; when he suffered, he did not threaten, rather, he delivered himself to him that judged him unjustly, who himself bore our sins in his body upon the tree.[13] He humbled himself, made obedient unto death, even the death of the Cross.[14] By whose stripe we are healed."[15] Lastly, he was mocked, spit upon, whipped, crowned with thorns, and being crucified with terrible ignominy and pain, he gave up his life to destroy the works of the devil, and to wipe away our sins. The law of God can witness, which prohibits and punishes all sin, indeed, it does not even leave one idle word unpunished.[16] How greatly does God abhor the terrible crimes when he cannot endure one idle word? "The law of our Lord is immaculate, the command of our Lord clear,"[17] detesting sin and darkness, for there can be no fellowship between light and darkness, justice and wickedness.[18] Hell can also witness what God has prepared for sinners, who when they had time, either neglected or refused to be washed with the blood of the immaculate Lamb. It is just that those who have committed an eternal sin should receive an eternal punishment. Still, it is horrible to consider what, and how

---

[8] 1 John 3:8.
[9] Phil. 2:6-7,
[10] 2 Cor. 8:9.
[11] Lk. 9:58.
[12] John 1:11.
[13] 1 Pet. 2:23-24.
[14] Phil. 2:8.
[15] 1 Pet. 2:24.
[16] Matt. 12:36.
[17] Ps. 18 (19):8-9.
[18] 2 Cor. 6:14.

great are the pains of hell. We will speak more about this in the last step.

Now, my soul, since God's hatred for sin is so great, if you love God above all things, it would behoove you to hate sin above all things. Be careful lest they deceive you, who make light of or excuse sin; take care lest you are deceived by false reasoning; for if sin does not displease you both in yourself and others, you do not love God, and if you do not love God, then you are ruined. Again, if you are grateful to Christ, how greatly you will count yourself in debt to his love, his labors, his blood, and death, who washed you from sin and reconciled you to his Father. How much of a burden will it be for you then, to suffer something for Christ, or in and with his grace to resist sin even unto blood for his sake? Lastly, if you cannot patiently endure the hell of eternal fire, then really, you should not patiently endure sin, but turn away from it as from the face of a snake, as well as from every light occasion or suspicion of it. So, let it be a firm and certain resolution to join the greatest hatred of sin with the greatest love of God.

CHAPTER II
Fire Perfects the Nobler Metals, and God Crowns the Good Works of Man

NOW the same fire does not destroy, but perfects and makes gold, silver, and precious stones more pure. This is because (as the Apostle explains), those metals signify good and perfect works which are approved by the fire of the divine judgment,[19] and have a great reward. God approves these works because they are his gifts, and "when he crowns our

---

[19] 1 Cor. 3:13.

The Sixth Step: A Consideration of Fire

merits, he crowns his gifts," as Augustine says.[20] For they are done by his command, assistance and power, and by the law and precepts which he has appointed.

Gold also indicates works of charity. How could works of charity not please God, when God himself is charity?[21] Silver indicates works of wisdom, namely the sort which instruct many to justice.[22] They are also very pleasing and acceptable to God, since the wisdom of God says: "He that will do and teach men likewise will be called great in the kingdom of heaven."[23] Precious stones are the works of a continent soul, which Sirach speaks of: "The worth of a continent soul cannot be measured."[24] This is why in the office of the Church, the Gospel on the pearl of great price is read in praise of holy virgins.[25] Now, how very greatly the purity of virginity is pleasing to God will be understood from the prophet Isaiah, who by God's appointment and in his name gave prophesy to such eunuchs as have castrated themselves for the sake of the kingdom of heaven. "I will give them a place in my house and within my walls, and a name better than sons and daughters; I will give an eternal name to them which will not perish."[26] St. Augustine speaks on this passage in his book *On Holy Virginity*, and says that it must be understood on holy virgins of either sex.[27] By the consensus of the doctors, these three sorts of works are rewarded with crowns of gold in the kingdom of heaven. For crowns of gold, namely certain rewards besides eternal life are given to martyrs, doctors, and virgins. It is given to martyrs for their excellent charity, because "No man has

---

[20] *Enerrat. In Ps.* lxx, 2,5.
[21] 1 Jn. 4:8.
[22] Dan. 12:3.
[23] Matt. 5:19.
[24] Sirach 26:20.
[25] *Missale Romanum*, de commun. Virg.
[26] Isa. 56:6.
[27] *De S. Virginitate* 24-25.

greater love than this, to give up his life for his friends."[28] To Teachers, for their excellent wisdom, of whom Daniel speaks: "They that instruct many to justice will shine as stars unto perpetual eternities;"[29] to Virgins, for their valuable chastity, for which reason the virgins in the Apocalypse are said to sing a new song that no man else could say: "These are the men who have not been defiled with women. For they are virgins and follow the Lamb wherever he shall go."[30]

Nevertheless, not only the charity of Martyrs, the wisdom of Teachers, and the purity of Virgins will not be approved by the fire of God's judgment, and fully rewarded; but also all other good works done in charity shall be esteemed as vessels of gold and endure that divine fire and receive their reward. For the Lord will say at the day of judgment: "Come ye blessed of my Father, possess the kingdom prepared from the foundation of the world;"[31] you who have given bread to the hungry, drink to the thirsty, lodging to strangers, clothing to the naked, and comfort to the sick and such as are in prison. The same Lord also promises that whosoever that whoever will give a cup of cold water out of charity only in the name of a disciple will not lose his reward.[32]

Do you understand, O my soul, how great a difference there is between works and works? Do you see how very stupid and miserable you are when you have time and place to easily purchase gold, silver, and precious stones, but instead seek after wood, grass and stubble with great labor? "O that you were wise and understood, and would prepare for your last end,"[33] when all these works will be examined

---

[28] Jn. 15:13.
[29] Dan. 12:3.
[30] Apoc. 14:3-4.
[31] Matt. 25:34.
[32] Matt. 10:42.
[33] Deut. 32:22, 29; Sirach 7:40.

and tried in the fire of God's judgment, and the former shall be raised and crowned, but the latter shall be burned to smoke and ashes. Why do you now choose that which doubtless you will be sorry to have chosen? Why do you not now condemn, while you profitably can, that which soon you will condemn without profit? If perhaps you do not see it now, seeing that the veil of present things hinders your eyes from beholding the clear and simple truth, pray to God, and say to him with great devotion like the blind man in the Gospel, "Lord grant that I may see,"[34] and with the prophet, "Unveil my eyes and I will consider the marvelous things of your law."[35] It is truly a marvel that works performed in charity become gold, silver and precious stones; but such as are not done in charity are turned to wood, grass and stubble.

CHAPTER III
Just as Fire Makes Dark Iron Bright; God Leads a Sinful Soul to Knowledge of the Truth

NOW we come to the consideration of another property of fire. To this point, we have learned from fire what God does with those who depart from this life with evil works or who arrive at the end of their life in good works. Now, by another similitude taken from the same fire we can understand what God works in those whom he calls to repentance from sin.

A sinful man is similar to iron, which as long as it is away from the fire is black, cold, hard, and heavy; but if it is put in the fire it becomes white, hot, soft, and light. Every

---

[34] Lk. 18:41.
[35] Ps. 118 (119):18.

sinner lacks the inward light and walks in darkness and thereby resembles the darkness of iron; although he seems skilled in knowledge and business, and excels in understanding and judgment of the same, yet he is blind in the judgment of true good and evil and is more miserable than any blind man. A blind man does not see, and so does not go out without a guide; but a sinful man thinks that he sees what he does not, or sees one thing for another, judging good to be evil and evil good, great to be little and little great, long to be short and short long; and as a result, he is always deceived in his choice.

The Apostle speaks this way in regard to the pagan idolaters: "Having their understanding obscured with darkness by the ignorance that is in them, because of the blindness of their heart."[36] This is what the Lord himself in the Gospel so often rebukes the Scribes and Pharisees, because they were blind, and leaders of the blind.[37] This is what the Prophet Isaiah says about the Jews of his time, "Hear, O deaf, and you blind men, behold and see,"[38] to whom he prophesied that Christ would come and open the eyes of the blind; and speaking of the New testament in the person of God, he adds, "And I will lead the blind into the way which they do not know, and in paths which they were unaware of ... I will make darkness light before them and crooked things straight."[39] Furthermore, the wicked will confess, after this life, that it is true, when their punishments will begin to open the eyes of their minds, which their sins had shut. They will say: "We have erred from the way of truth, and the light of justice has not shined upon us, and the sun of understanding did not rise upon

---

[36] Eph. 4:18.
[37] Matt. 15:14; Lk. 6:39.
[38] Isa. 42:18.
[39] Isa. 42:18.

The Sixth Step: A Consideration of Fire 79

us."[40] Nor should there be any marvel, although they are bind which are turned away from God in understanding and will, "God is light and no darkness is in him."[41] Thus, the same Apostle concludes, "The man that says he is in the light and hates his brother is in darkness even to now.... But he that hates his brother is in darkness, and walks in darkness, and does not know where he goes; because the darkness has blinded his eyes."[42]

That they are turned from God who is Light is not the only cause of blindness in sinners, rather, it is also that "their malice has blinded them."[43] For love, hatred, anger, envy, and similar passions of the mind, which are embraced under the name of malice, so blind the mind that it cannot seethe truth; and they are as colored glasses which make white things appear to be red, or else so framed that they make great things seems mall, or small things seem great, things far off seem near, and things near seem far off. A man who is in love thinks the thing he loves to be most beautiful, profitable, and necessary, and that it must be gained before all things. Again, a man that hates the same thing, judges it most deformed, unprofitable, evil, and hurtful, and to be forsaken before all other things. Now, if this dark and deformed iron were put into the fire, that is, if the sinner began to turn away from sin and turn toward God, following the saying of the prophet, "Come to him and be illuminated,"[44] then he begins, little by little, to receive the light and to see truth in that light, according to the saying of the same prophet, "In your light we shall see light."[45] Then, breaking the colored glasses of passion into pieces, and taking the crystal clear charity, he will regard eternal things

---

[40] Wis. 5:6.
[41] 1 Jn. 1:5.
[42] 1 Jn. 2:9, 11.
[43] Wis. 2:21.
[44] Ps. 33 (34):6.
[45] Ps. 25 (26):10.

as great, and temporal things a small and of scant importance, as they truly are.

Then he will see clearly that no created beauty is to be compared with that Light of wisdom and truth which is God and in God. In this way, he may cry out with st. Augustine: "Late have I loved you, O ancient beauty but ever new, late have I loved you."[46] Now, since Christ says, "You will know the truth and the truth shall set you free,"[47] he that is illuminated with the light of truth in this way, and freed from the bonds of concupiscence, covetousness, ambition, and other passions, may rejoice with the prophet and say, "You, O Lord, have broken my bonds, I will sacrifice to you an oblation of praise, and I will invoke the name of the Lord."[48]

Chapter IV

A Burning Fire Welds Cold Iron; the Grace of God Restores Strength to Men's Words and Deeds

FIRE does not only cause iron which is dark to become bright, but also that which is cold to become hot, nay more, so fiery and burning that it seems to be fire itself. Our Lord is great and his power is great, which takes a man that is cold and fearful by nature, who can neither speak nor dare to embark on anything that is just a little difficult, enkindles the fire of charity, and causes him to be bolder than a lion, who terrifies all by his roar, conquers all in war, for whom nothing is difficult, nothing seems arduous, and he can say with Paul the Apostle after that fire was forcefully lit, "I can

---

[46] *Confess.* 10, 27.
[47] Jn. 8:32.
[48] Ps. 115 (116):7-8.

do all things in him who strengthens me."[49]

Now, let us speak particularly on this efficacy of fire, and first let us briefly treat of the efficacy of words and then the efficacy of deeds. There are today, and always have been many preachers of God's Word in the Church. What then, is the cause that in spite of the exhortations and crying out of so many men, so few are converted? Truly, every day in Lent in the great towns, twenty, thirty, or forty preachers speak, and still, when Lent is finished, there appears almost no change in the manners of the citizens and townsmen; the same vices, the same sins, the same coldness, the same looseness is still seen. I can find no other cause for this except that, although for the most part, learned, eloquent, and copious sermons are preached, nevertheless, the soul is wanting, the life is wanting, the fire is wanting. In a word, that great charity is wanting which alone can light a fire in the words of the speakers and bring their words to life, and change the hearts of the hearers. I do not say that many preachers do not have loudness of voice and action of body; for guns without either bullet or stone make a loud noise when they are shot, but to no purpose. What is desired is that they would show great zeal for God and the salvation of souls, not as a feint, but truly, not strained, but naturally flowing from the fountain of the heart. St. Peter was ignorant of rhetoric—he was only an expert in sailing his boat and in casting and fixing his nets; yet, as soon as the Holy Spirit descended upon him in a fiery tongue, and replenished him with fervent charity, he presently began to speak so powerfully, fervently, and effectively in the midst of the city of Jerusalem, that with one sermon he converted many thousands to believe and do penance.[50] Yet, we do not read in his sermons that he used a strained voice or a wearisome motion of the body.

---

[49] Phil. 4:13.
[50] Act. 2:14 *seqq*.

St. Bonaventure relates that St. Francis was unlearned, and that he never studied the science of rhetoric. Nevertheless, when he preached to the people, he was heard as an angel from heaven;[51] for his words were like fire inflaming the heart, and, on one occasion after lunch, when he spoke all of the sudden a few words to the people, they were all so moved to repentance that it seemed like it was Good Friday.[52] From where did such great fruit proceed from so few words? Truly, because that holy preacher was "like a burning coal, and his words as a burning torch," as Sirach writes of Elijah.[53] We have the written sermons of St. Vincent, St. Bernardine, and some other saints, which scarce any will undertake to read, because of the very plain style which is found in them, and yet we know that by their preaching many thousands of men have been converted to God, and themselves were ever heard with incredible fanfare and attention, because their plain and simple words proceeded from fiery and zealous hearts.

Furthermore, the efficacy of this divine fire is shown as much in deeds as in words. God determined to subdue Rome, the chief city of the Empire and mistress of the nations unto himself through St. Peter the Apostle. He also determined to destroy the idols of the world, to raise the standard of the Cross, to change laws and customs, and to overthrow the tyranny of the devil by sending the rest of the Apostles, some into Ethiopia, some into India, some into Scythia, some into the farthest parts of Brittany. If anyone had foretold these things to the Apostles while they were fishing in the lake of Genesareth, or when they fled away and hid during our Lord's Passion, they would have seemed as dreams or old wive's tales. Just the same, immediately after they did all of these things by no other force than by

---

[51] *Chronicles of the Friars Minor*, c. 30.
[52] *Vita S. Francesci*, c. 2.
[53] Sirach 48:1.

the fire of charity which the Holy Spirit enkindled in their hearts. For charity casts out fear,[54] suffers all things, hopes all things,[55] thinks all things possible and cries out with the Apostle: "I can do all things in him that strengthens me."[56]

So that we see by the work and labor of these men, armed with charity alone, idolatry was in short order extinguished throughout the world, churches were everywhere built to the honor of Christ, and the standard of the Cross, without an army, or provision of war, erected in all kingdoms.

Chapter V
Fire Makes Hard Iron Soft; the Grace of God Conquers the Hardness of the Heart

FIRE also has a property to cause hard iron to become so soft that it may be easily thinned and extended into plates and brought to any form. Fire has great power over iron, but God has a greater power over the obstinate and hard hearts of mortal men. Let us listen to St. Bernard in his book *On Consideration,* "It is only a hard heart which does not abhor itself, because it does not feel. What then is a hard heart? It is that which is neither struck with compunction, softened with piety, or moved with prayer. It does not care for threats, and is hardened by punishments. It is ungrateful for benefits, and disbelieves counsel. ... It is that which fears neither God nor man."[57] Pharaoh is a witness that all of this is absolutely true, since the more he was punished by God, the more he was hardened, and the more God's mercy

---

[54] 1 Jn. 4:8.
[55] 1 Cor. 13:7.
[56] Phil. 4:13.
[57] *De Consideratione* 1, 2.

appeared in removing his punishment, the more determined he was to despise and scorn God. Now, when our Lord is pleased to enkindle one spark of the fire of his true love in a heart—no matter how hardened—it immediately softens and begins to melt like wax, so that no strength of that long obstinacy or hardness will resist it; rather, it immediately comes to pass that the heart of stone becomes a heart of flesh, and from frozen snow, by the warm breath of the Lord, waters will flow.[58] We have an example in the Gospel from that woman who was a sinner in a city, would not stop sinning by the admonitions of her brother, rebukes of her sister, or the honor of her family, nor even her own shame. Nevertheless, one ray of Christ piercing her heart, and there the spark of divine love was enkindled, and so strangely altered her, so that being a noble woman, she was not ashamed to cast herself at Christ's feet. Weeping, with her tears she bathed them and with her hair instead of a towel she wiped them. Frequently she most lovingly kissed them, and with a most precious and sweet-smelling ointment she anointed them, signifying thereby that from then on, she meant to dedicate herself and all she possessed to the service of Christ.[59] As a result, she deserved to hear the Lord's saying, "Many sins have been forgiven her, because she has loved much."[60]

Yet it only seems right to lay down another example from a later time. William, the Duke of Aquitaine, lived in the time of St. Bernard; a strong-willed man and very obstinate in defending Anacletus, the Antipope, against Innocent the true Pope. He banished all the Catholic bishops from his country, and swore an oath that he would never be at peace with them; and because all men knew how obdurate he was in wickedness and cruelty, as well as

---

[58] Ps. 147:18.
[59] Lk. 7:37 *et seqq.*
[60] Lk. 7:47.

terrible for his pride; there was not a man that dared to admonish him. It pleased God by his servant Bernard to visit the hard heart of this man and to kindle a great spark of divine love therein. Right away he went from a lion to a lamb, from proud to humble, and from obstinate to most obedient. At only one word of St. Bernard, he gave a friendly embrace to the Bishop of Poitiers, and with his own hand placed him in his chair. What seemed to surpass all admiration, is when he sought from a certain hermit a remedy for his soul on account of the sins he had committed, and the hermit commanded him to wear a brass breastplate next to his skin, buckled in such a way that it could never be taken off, and he obeyed without hesitation, and did it. Being sent by the hermit to the Pope for absolution, he went. Now the Pope suspected that he did not truly repent, or meant to try his patience, so he commanded him to go on pilgrimage to Jerusalem to demand absolution from the Patriarch of that city. William undertook the journey without delay, and fulfilled the Pope's command. Lastly, from a powerful prince he became a humble monk, so that in that age there was hardly anyone found to surpass him in humility, patience, poverty, devotion, and piety. "This is the change of the right hand of the most high."[61] This is the force of the divine fire, against which no hard heart can resist.

Chapter VI
Fire Thins Heavy Things; the Grace of God Directs Souls in the Way of Justice.

THERE remains the last property of fire, which is to thin

---

[61] Ps. 76:11.

heavy things, and make it an easy business to raise them up again. This is the reason why men that do not burn with the fire of divine love are heavy of heart, and the prophet says to them, "How long are you heavy of heart? Why do you love vanity and chase after a lie?"[62] This is also the reason why "the body that is corrupted weighs down the soul,"[63] and "a heavy yoke upon the children of Adam, from the day of their coming from their mother's womb, until the day of their burial, unto the mother of all."[64] What this heavy burden is, which in this mortal body so weighs down the soul, the same author declares a little later, when he adds, "wrath, envy, tumult, fear, anger,"[65] and similar things, commonly called the passions of the mind. These so depress the mind of man that it beholds nothing but the earth, to which it cleaves, in such a sort that it cannot climb up to seek God, nor run quickly the way of his commandments. Now, when the fire of God begins to inflame it from on high, immediately those passions begin to diminish and be mortified, and this heavy burden to grow lighter; and if the heat increases it will so unburden the heart that it may fly up like a dove, and say with the Apostle, "Our conversation is in heaven."[66] Being enlarged with this fire, it may say with David, "I have run the way of your commandments, when you have expanded my heart."[67] Certainly, after our Savior said, "I come to cast fire on the earth, and what will I except that it be set ablaze?"[68] we have seen many so enlightened that they have completely forsaken the love of honor, pleasure, and wealth, and have said to Christ ascending to

---

[62] Ps. 4:3.
[63] Wis. 9:15.
[64] Sirach 40:1.
[65] *Ibid.* 4.
[66] Phil. 3:20.
[67] Ps. 118 (119):32.
[68] Lk. 12:49.

heaven, "draw us after you."[69]

This caused so many monasteries to be built, so many migrants to the desert, so many companies of virgins to be established, who did not only run the way of the commandments with ease, but also ascended unto the way of the counsels: "To follow the Lamb wherever he will go."[70]

O blessed fire, who does not consume, but gives light! If you consume anything, you merely consume a harmful humor, lest it would prevent life. Who will cause me to be inflamed with this fire which, with the light of true wisdom, expels the darkness of ignorance and blindness of an erroneous conscience? This fire which changes the coldness of sloth, indevotion, and negligence into the heat of love, so that it will never suffer my heart to be hardened, but with the heat thereof to be softened and made devout; the fire which removes heavy burden of earthly cares and desires, so that with the wings of holy contemplation, with which charity is nourished and increased, my heart shall be lifted up in such a way that I may say with the prophet, "Make joyful the soul of your servant, because to you, O Lord, I have lifted up my soul."[71]

---

[69] Cant. 1:3.
[70] Apoc. 14:4.
[71] Ps. 85 (86):4.

THE SEVENTH STEP
From the Consideration of the Heaven, Namely the Sun, Moon and Stars

CHAPTER I
The Sun, as the Tabernacle of the Most High and Exceedingly Beautiful God

E will not labor much in this place from the consideration of heaven to frame for ourselves a step to contemplate God, for we have the royal prophet going before us, who says, "the heavens show forth the glory of God, and the firmament declares the works of his hands."[1] Now because there are two seasons, namely the day and the night, in which we may, from the consideration of heaven, ascend to God with the wings of contemplation, David writes, "He put his tabernacle in the sun, and himself as a bridegroom, coming forth from his bride-chamber. He rejoiced as a giant to run the way, his coming forth from the top of heaven, and his recourse even to the top thereof; neither is there that can hide himself from his heat."[2] He writes on the latter in another Psalm: "I shall see the heavens, the works of your fingers, the moon and the stars, which you have founded."[3]

Let us start with the first season. The Holy Spirit sings four praises about the sun which we look upon daily, by the mouth of David. First, it is God's tabernacle; secondly, it is

---
[1] Ps. 18 (19):1.
[2] Ps. 18 (19):6-7.
[3] Ps. 8:4.

exceedingly beautiful; thirdly, that it always runs very swiftly without stopping; fourthly, that it especially manifests its power by giving light and heat. Sirach writes on account of all these, "Admirable vessel, work of the most high; great is our Lord who made it."[4]

In the first place, God, who framed all things, has put his tabernacle in the sun, as in the noblest of his creation, i.e. that among all corporeal things he has chosen the sun as a princely palace or divine sanctuary to dwell in. God truly fills heaven and earth,[5] and the heaven and heaven of heavens does not contain him; and yet he is said principally to dwell there, whereby working marvels he shows greater signs of his presence. Now, because the Hebrew text says "He has put a tabernacle for the sun in them, namely, in the heavens, we gather from this passage of the psalm another excellence of the sun which is not opposed to the former. The sun is a great thing, and God has prepared a most spacious, beautiful, and noble palace for it. He would have heaven itself be the palace of the sun, that it would freely move and work, and the sun to be the palace of God the supreme ruler. Just the same, we know the great excellence of the sun because of the very fact heaven is its tabernacle, so we may know the great excellence of God, because the sun is his tabernacle; an admirable vessel, and nothing found among corporeal things which is more wonderful than it is.

Next, David, so as to show the excellent beauty of the sun by things already known, he compared it with a bridegroom emerging from his bedchamber, for men never adorn themselves more, or seek more to show their beauty and excellence than when they are bridegrooms, for then they greatly desire to please the eyes of their spouse, whom they love most dearly. Yet, if we were so close to the sun as to see what and how great it is, we should not then need to

---

[4] Sirach 43:2, 5.
[5] Jer. 23:24.

use the resemblance of a bridegroom to conceive its incredible beauty. Truly, the beauty of colors depends upon light, and the light failing, the beauty of colors soon fades away. So, nothing is more beautiful than light. This is why God, who is beauty itself, would be called light. "God is the light, and there is not any darkness in him."[6] Next, among corporeal things there is nothing so bright as the sun, and as a result, nothing is more beautiful than it. The beauty of lower things, especially of men, shortly fades, but the beauty of the sun is never extinguished nor diminished, rather, it always shines upon all with an equal brightness. Do we not perceive how all things rejoice at the rising of the sun? Not only do men rejoice, but even the sweet winds blow, the flowers open, the plants rise, birds delight in song. Thus, when the angel told old and blind Tobit, "Joy be to you always," answered, "What joy is it to me when I sit in darkness and do not see the light of heaven?"[7]

Well now, my soul, think to yourself; if the created sun brings joy to all things by its rising, what will the uncreated Son do (which is without comparison more beautiful and bright) when to the clean of heart he shall rise not to be seen for short while, but for all eternity! How sorrowful and unhappy will that hour be to the wicked, when they will be sent away to be buried in eternal darkness, where neither the uncreated nor the created sun will ever shine! How great the joy will that soul have to whom the Father of lights will say, "Enter into the joy of your Lord"?[8]

---

[6] 1 John 1:5.
[7] Tob. 5:11-12.
[8] Matt. 25:21.

Chapter II
From the Course of the Sun the Greatness of God Appears

THEN, David extolled the course of the sun, which is also very admirable, "He has rejoiced as a giant to run his way."[9]

A powerful giant, if he would extend his steps in accord with his stature, and run as fast as his strength would afford, he will go a long way in a short time. Truly, the prophet, having compared the sun to a bridegroom so as to declare its beauty, he later compares it to a giant so that by the resemblance he might show in some way how fast its stride is. Now, albeit he had not compared it to a giant, but to the flight of birds and arrows, or to the winds and lightning, yet should it have been far from the thing indeed. If that is true which we see with our eyes, namely, that the sun makes its course around the earth in twenty-four hours, and if the measure of the suns orb exceeds almost without comparison the measure of the earth, and if the measure of the earth contains about twenty thousand miles, all which is most true, it necessarily follows that the sun, at every hour, moves many thousands of miles; and why say I every hour, nay every quarter of an hour, indeed, almost every minute? Whosoever observes the rising or setting of the sun, in an open horizon, as at sea or in a plain field, will perceive the whole body of the sun moves above the horizon in less space than an eighth of an hour. And yet, the diameter of the sun's body is much greater than the diameter of the earth, which, notwithstanding, contains seven thousand miles. I myself was once eager to know in what space of time the sun set at sea, at the beginning thereof I began to read the Psalm

---

[9] Ps. 18 (19):6.

Miserere mei Deus,[10] and scarce had I read it twice over before the sun had completely set. As a result, it must be the case that the sun passed through far more space than seven miles in the short time in which I said the *Miserere* twice. Who would believe this, unless certain reason proved it? And now, if anyone were to say that this body, which is so swiftly moved, is much greater than the whole earth, and that its motion is performed without ceasing or weariness, so that God should so command, it might continue for all eternity; surely, if he were not insensible, he could not but marvel at the infinite power of God. Sirach rings true, when he says, "That this is an admirable vessel, the work of the most high, and great is our Lord that made it."[11]

CHAPTER III
The Sun Gives Light and Heat; God Also Gives Wisdom and Charity

THE EFFICACY of the sun's light and heat remains, about which David says, "And there is no one who can hide himself from its heat." This one bright body, being placed in the midst of the world, looks over all the stars, all the air, all the sea, and all the earth, and with its life-giving heat it causes all plants, all crops, all trees throughout the world to blossom and bear fruit; and under the earth it also produces every type of metals. This is why James compares the sun to God: "Every best and perfect gift is from above, descending from the Father of Lights, with whom is no change, nor shadow of alteration."[12] Truly the sun is the father of corporeal light, as God is the Father of spiritual light; yet

---

[10] Ps. 50 (51).
[11] Sirach 43:2, 5.
[12] Jas. 1:17.

there are three important differences between God and the sun.

First, the sun needs continual change to give light and heat to the whole world; but God is completely everywhere and needs no change. Therefore, St. James says, "With whom is no change."

Secondly, for this reason, the sun always changes places, and through successions causes it to be day for some men and night for others, shines upon some, is darkened for others. Now, God is never changed, and yet is present to everyone, so St. James adds, "There is with him no shadow of alteration."

Lastly, and what is the greatest of all, from the sun (the father of corporeal light) all things proceed which grow upon the earth. Now, those things are good, but they are neither the best nor the perfect, rather, small, temporal and transitory; they do not make men good, and they can be used badly by those who wish to, and a great many turn them to their ruin. God, on the other hand, from the Father of spiritual light, "every best gift and every perfect gift descends," whereby the possessors of it become better and more perfect. No one can abuse these gifts, and whoever perseveres in them to the end will come to that true happiness which is a state of all good things perfectly united together.

So my soul, seek what these best and perfect gifts are, which come down from the Father of Light. When you have discovered them, see to it that you strive to obtain them with all of your strength. Now, you will not need to look far, since the sun sufficiently shows them to you. The sun by its light and heat, which are the gifts of the Father of corporeal light, produce all things; so also the best gifts and perfect gifts which are from above, and come down from God the true Father of Light, and the light of wisdom and ordinance of charity. The light of wisdom (which makes us truly wise

The Seventh Step: A Consideration of the Heavens 95

and leads us to the heavenly Fountain of Wisdom), teaches us to scorn corporeal things and to esteem eternal ones; it teaches us, "Do not trust in the uncertainty of riches but in the living God."[13] It teaches us not to make a country out of this exile, nor to love this pilgrimage, but to bear it. Lastly, it teaches us to hold this life in patience, which is so full of dangers and temptation, and death in desire, because, "Blessed are the dead that die in our Lord."[14] The ordinance of true charity is to love God without end, who is the end of all desires; and to love other things insofar as they will be necessary to obtain that happiness. In truth, there is no one among the children of men who will overturn order in the care of his body so as to love his health with measure and a bitter dink without measure, seeing that he knows that the former is the end and the latter is but the means to obtain that end.

Why does it come to pass that so many who would be considered wise keep no measure in amassing riches, in seeking the pleasures of the flesh, and in obtaining degrees of honor, as if these goods were the purpose of the heart of man? And why is the love of God and the seeking after eternal happiness scorned by those in difficulties as if these were the means to an end, and not the end of all means? Truly, the reason is because they have the wisdom of this world, and not the wisdom which is from above, coming down from the Father of Light. Now, since their love is not orderly, as a result it is not true love, which cannot be but orderly; for they are full of avarice, which is not from God, but from the world. Now you, my soul, while you are a pilgrim from your country, and among enemies, which besiege true wisdom and charity, and call subtlety wisdom, and avarice frugality, weep from the bottom of your heart to the Father of Light, that it would please him to cause those

---

[13] 1 Tim. 6:17.
[14] Apoc. 14:13.

best and perfect gifts, namely the light of true wisdom and the heat of orderly charity, to descend into your heart; and so being replenished with them, it may run without stumbling on the path of God's commandments, and come to that country where they drink of the fountain of wisdom and live by the pure milk of charity.

Chapter IV

As the Moon Receives its Light from the Sun, So the Soul Truly Joined to God, Receives Pure Light

I COME now to the period of night, in which the heaven makes a step for us to ascend to God by the moon and stars. David speaks in this way: "Since I will see your heavens, the work of your fingers, the moon and the stars which you have founded."[15] If we could see heaven itself, the prophet would not have said, as if he were explaining what he had already set down, "the moon and the stars which you founded," and rightly, if our senses reach to heaven itself, or if we could investigate its nature and qualities by certain reason we should have an excellent ladder to ascend unto God. We know that there are some who defined the nature of the heavens by the motion of the stars to be a fifth element, simple, incorruptible, and always circularly moving; and we know that there have been others who also hold heaven to be the element of fire, not moved circularly and in some parts corruptible. Now, we do not seek after opinion, but certain knowledge or doctrine of faith, so that we my thereby construct a firm ladder to know God. From the moon and the stars which we see, we will set up a ladder with the prophet, as we have already done for the sun,

---

[15] Ps. 8:4.

which is the light and beginning of other lights.

The moon has two properties which can help us ascend unto God and serve him. First, the closer it comes to the sun, the brighter it is in the higher part which looks to heaven, and darkened in its lower part, which looks to earth. Now, when it is opposite the sun, it shines as full to the inhabitants of the earth, and has no light in the higher part towards heaven. This property of the moon can teach men how careful they must be of their nearness, subjection, and union with God, the true Father of lights. The moon signifies man, the sun, God. When the moon faces opposite the sun, there with her light borrowed from the sun, she only beholds the earth, and turns her back as it were, to heaven. As a result, she then appears very beautiful to the inhabitants of the earth, but deformed to those of heaven. Even so, men, when they are far from God, as the prodigal son who departed from his father and went into a far country, then they abuse the light of reason, which they received from him, to behold the earth alone, and are altogether occupied in getting the wealth of it. Then the children of this world are accounted wise and happy; but of the heavenly citizens they are esteemed poor, blind, and naked, as well as miserable.[16] On the other hand, when the moon is under the sun or near to it, then it shines in the higher part, and only looks to heaven, turning, as it were, her back to the earth and vanishing from the sight of men. Even so, when a sinner begins to return to virtue, and to be truly subject unto God, the true sun of souls, by humility and joined unto him by charity, then will he fulfil that which the Apostle teaches, "Seek the things that are above, where Christ sits on the right hand of God, and mind the things that are above, not the things that are upon the earth,"[17] and he shall taste those things which are above, not which are

---

[16] Apoc. 3:17.
[17] Col. 3:1-2.

upon the earth, and he will be scorned by the foolish, and be counted as dead. Truly such a man is dead to the world, and his life is hidden with Christ in God, and when Christ his life will appear, then he will also appear with Christ in glory, as the Apostle also relates.[18]

This is also why, as St. Augustine notes,[19] the Pasch of the Lord could not be celebrated correctly either in the Old Law or in the New until the full moon was past, namely, until the moon which at the full is opposite, begins by waning to return to union with the sun. For God means to show by this celestial sign how man, who was opposite to God by his wickedness, would begin to return unto God by the Passion and resurrection of Christ, and to seek to unite himself to his grace by the merits of Christ.

Now, my soul, if perhaps by God's grace you will find yourself subjected to the Father of lights by true humility, do not imitate fools who are changed just like the moon; rather, emulate the wise, who last, just like the sun, as Sirach witnesses.[20] For the moon recedes from union as quickly as it hastens toward it; but if you are wise, do not abandon grace once it has been received, do not depart from it, since you can find nothing better in any place. Nor do you know, if you will have receded of you own will, whether it will be granted to return again at another time. He that promised pardon and grace to the penitent has not promised the gift of repentance or a long life to you. So, you may turn your back to the earth without fear, and behold your sun. Rest, delight, and remain in him. Say, with St. Peter, "It is good for us to be here,"[21] and with the holy martyr Ignatius of Antioch, "It is better for me to live with Christ than to rule

---

[18] Ibid., 3-4.
[19] *Ep.* 55 *ad Januarium*.
[20] Sirach 27:12.
[21] Matt. 17:4.

the earth."[22] Let the judgment of men who savor the world count as nothing. A man is not approved because the world commends him, but because God commends him.

Chapter V
The Moon Illuminating the Night and Leaving Us for a Time in Darkness Is a Figure of Divine Grace

IT IS another habit of the moon, which God customarily preserves with his elect. The moon is in charge of the night, just as the sun the day, as Moses says in Genesis,[23] and David in the Psalms.[24] Now, the sun shines throughout the day; at night the moon sometimes casts a great light, sometimes a small one, and sometimes the darkness is without any consolation of any light. God, like the sun, always shines with perpetual brightness upon the holy angels and the souls of the blessed, for whom the day is perpetual (there will be no night there, as St. John says in the Apocalypse).[25] The night of our pilgrimage and exile, however, in which "we walk by faith and not by sight,"[26] and come to Holy Scripture like "a lit candle in a dark place,"[27] God, like the moon, sometimes visits and shines upon our hearts, and sometimes he leaves us in the darkness of desolation. Nevertheless, my soul, you should not be too sorrowful, even if you do not enjoy the light of consolation, nor should you rejoice overmuch if shortly after you enjoy the light of consolation and devotion. God is as the moon

---

[22] *Ep. Ad Rom.* 6.
[23] Gen. 1:16.
[24] Ps. 135 (136):8-9.
[25] Apoc. 21:25.
[26] 2 Cor. 5:7.
[27] 2 Pet. 1:19.

and not the sun in the light of this world. Not only does he appear unto us poor and imperfect creatures, sometimes as a moon full of the light of consolation and sometimes leaving us devoid of all light in the horror and densest darkness of the night; for the Apostle Paul, "the vessel of election,"[28] who was "taken into the third heaven and heard secret words which it is not permitted for a man to speak,"[29] says, "I am replenished with consolation, I do exceedingly abound in joy in all of our tribulation,"[30] and at other times he sighs and laments, saying, "I see another law in my members, fighting the law of my mind, and captivating me in the law of sin that is in my members. Unhappy man that I am, who shall deliver me from the body of this death?"[31] And he says to the Corinthians, "We will not have you ignorant, brethren, about our tribulation which has taken place in Asia, that we were pressed above measure, above our power, for that it was tedious unto us even to live."[32] Thus, as St. John Chrysostom notes, God deals with all his saints, namely, not suffering them to have continual tribulations, nor to enjoy continual consolations, but to entwine the life of the just, as it were, with an admirable variety both from adversities and prosperity.

---

[28] Act. 9:15.
[29] 2 Cor. 12:2, 4.
[30] 2 Cor. 7:4.
[31] Rom. 7:23-24.
[32] 2 Cor. 1:8.

CHAPTER VI
The Arrangement and Harmony of the Stars Presents an Image of the Heavenly Hierarchy

THE STARS remain among the adornments of heaven, about which Sirach speaks, "the glory of the stars is the beauty of heaven," but he adds, "Our Lord giving light to the world on high."[33] Whatever the beauty there is in the stars, the sun, and the moon proceeds from God, the Father of Light, nor does the sun by day or moon and stars by night give light, rather, it is the Lord that dwells on high, who by the sun, moon and stars gives light to the world. It is He, who as Baruch says, "sends forth light and it goes, and has called it and it obeys him with trembling. And the stars have given light in their vigils, and rejoiced; they were called, and they said, Here we are; and with cheerfulness they have shined unto him that made them."[34] The infinite power of God is signified by such words, which, with incredible ease, produced, and adorned bodies so vast and beautiful, and caused them to work. What "calling a thing" is to us, is for God to create in the word. For he calls things which do not exist, and by calling, he causes them to be.

Now, for the stars to say, "we are here," is nothing other than to come into being and work on the spot at the voice of the one commanding their existence. And to shine unto him that made them with cheerfulness is to obey their maker with such readiness, that it seems as if in obeying him they were greatly pleased and delighted. Now surely, it is a marvelous thing that the stars, moving so speedily and continually, and some performing their course so slowly,

---

[33] Sirach 43:10.
[34] Bar. 3:33.

and some so swiftly in their region; yet they always keep such measure and proportion together, that from it arises a very sweet and pleasing harmony. God speaks about this harmony in Job when he says, "Who will declare the manner of the heavens, and who will cause the harmony of heaven to sleep?"[35] This is not the harmony of voices or sounds heard with corporeal ears, but the harmony of proportion in the motions of the stars, heard only with the ear of the heart. Now, all the stars of the firmament pass with the like speed about the whole orbit of the heavens in twenty-four hours, and the seven stars which are called planets, or wandering stars, are said with different motions, some urged on faster and some slower, so that the stars of the firmament appear to bear the plainsong (to use common terminology), and the planets to make a sweet and continual kind of counterpoint. Now these things are above us, and this harmony is heard only by those who are in heaven and understand the reasons for these motions. The stars also keep a just measure always in turning around; and therefore, they seem like in the manner of honest virgins skillful at dancing, always to make the most joyful dances[36] in heaven.

Now you, my soul, go up a little higher if you can, and by the great brightness of the sun, the beauty of the moon, the multitude and variety of the other lights, the admirable harmony of heaven, and delightful dancing of the stars, think what it will be to behold God above heaven, namely that sun "which inhabits light not accessible,"[37] to behold the Virgin Queen of Heaven, who being "fair as the moon,"[38] brings joy to the whole city of God; to behold the choirs and

---

[35] Job 38:37.
[36] Translator's note: The word here is *choreas*, which has a double meaning, not only a dance, but also used a planetary movement, but the meaning is lost in English.
[37] 1 Tim. 6:16.
[38] Cant. 6:9.

The Seventh Step: A Consideration of the Heavens

orders of angels, which being more in number and brighter than the stars, adorn the heaven of heaven; to behold the souls of the saints among the companies of angels, as planets among the stars of the firmament. Lastly, to hear the songs of praise, and that eternal Alleluia with consonant voices to resound most sweetly in the streets of that city. In this way it will come to pass that neither the beauty of heaven will seem great to you, nor the things under heaven, which are very small and altogether of no value, will be judged as contemptible and despicable.

THE EIGHTH STEP
From the Consideration of the Rational Soul

Chapter I
The Soul is the Created Spirit; God Is the Uncreated Spirit and Creator of All Things

O this point we have passed through all corporeal things, while we intended from the contemplation of created things to ascend to the Creator. Now, we find the soul of man, surpassing the dignity of all bodies to be in the lowest rank of spiritual substances, between which and God there is nothing apart from the hierarchies and orders of angels.

Moreover, the human soul has such a resemblance with God its maker, that truly I do not know an easier way for a man to climb up to know God than from a consideration of his own soul. Consequently, God will not hold a man inexcusable if he does not have the knowledge of God, since he is able—by God's help—draw it out from the knowledge of his own soul without difficulty.[1]

First, the soul of man is a spirit. The Holy Fathers expound the words of Genesis in this way, "The Lord God formed man from the slime of the earth and breathed into his face the breath of life,"[2] and that of Tobit, "Command my spirit to be received,"[3] as well as Ecclesiastes, "Let the dust

---

[1] Rom. 1:20.
[2] Gen. 2:7.
[3] Tob. 3:6.

return into its earth, and the spirit return to God who gave it."[4] Now, although the word "spirit" can also mean the wind, as it is said in the Psalms, "the spirit of gales,"[5] and in the Gospel, "the spirit breathes where it will and you hear his voice,"[6] nevertheless, there is no doubt that the spirit of storms is a very frail body, which on account of its frailty, imitates a spiritual nature more than any other body you like. Now, the human soul is properly a spirit, not a body. It is not produced from matter, rather, it is created by God, nor is there any controversy about this among Catholics.

Here then, begins the excellence of the soul and its resemblance to God. "God is a spirit, and they who adore him must adore him in spirit and in truth."[7] Now, although God is a spirit, and the soul of man is also a spirit, nevertheless, God is an uncreated spirit, the soul a created spirit from which it follows that there is an infinite difference between that spirit which is the soul and that Spirit which is God. Just as the soul may rejoice for being a spiritual substance, and by that fact is higher than the heavens and the stars in nobility of nature, so also she should be humbled before God, her creator, because she is made of nothing, and without him, of herself is nothing.

Chapter II
The Soul is Immortal; God Eternal

THE HUMAN SOUL is a simple spirit, and as a result immortal; it has nothing within itself that can dissolve it, or cause it to perish. Yet, as it has the privilege above the souls of wild

---

[4] Eccl. 12:7.
[5] Ps. 148:8.
[6] John 3:8.
[7] John 4:24.

animals, which die with the body, so it should likewise admire and reverence the excellence of the Creator, who is not only immortal, but also eternal. There was a time when the soul of man did not exist, and it came into being by the will of God alone, and further, may likewise be reduced to nothing, according to God's pleasure, although in itself it has no cause of corruption. In this way, the Apostle of God rightly says, "Who alone has immortality,"[8] because God is the only being who cannot be dissolved by any force, any chance, or reason, since he is being itself, the very light and font of being and life.

Chapter III
The Soul is Endowed with Reason; God is Light and Understanding

THIRDLY, the human soul has been endowed with the light of understanding; it knows not only colors and tastes, odors and sounds, heat and chill, hard and soft as well as other things of this sort which are clear to the senses of the body; but it also judges in regard to substance, and things not only individually, but also as a whole. It not only knows the present, but can even guess at the future and by running climbs up to heaven, penetrates the abyss, scrutinizes effects from their causes, and from the effects returns to the causes. Lastly, by the light of reason, it ascends to God who "dwells in light inaccessible."[9] St. John says of this light in his Gospel, "It was the true light which enlightens every man that comes into the world."[10] David in the Psalms, "The light of your countenance, O Lord, is sealed upon us," and "do not

---

[8] 1 Tim. 6:16.
[9] 1 Tim. 6:16.
[10] John 1:9.

become as a horse and mule, which have no understanding."[11]

Great is this dignity of the soul, whereby a man is like God, and not the animals. From there we may and must consider the infinite eminence and sublimity of God. Although the soul is endowed with the light of understanding, God is light and understanding. The soul runs from the cause to the effect, and from the effect to the cause, and obtains knowledge with great labor. God sees all things at once, and perfectly together. The soul understands things which are, and so her knowledge depends upon things; God, by his understanding causes things to exist, and as a result, their existence depends upon his knowledge. The soul conjectures in some way, in regard to future events; God sees always all things in the future, as plainly as things in the past or present. The soul is in need of many things to exercise the gift of understanding, such as object, species, phantasm, and the like; God is in need of nothing, for his essence is all things to him.

Lastly, the soul, while it is in the body, cannot properly see God, angels or itself or any substance truly, however corporeal; it also does not know many things and is deceived, conjecturing too much by opinion, and understanding little by demonstration. Still, God knows all things, without conjecture of error, for "all things are naked and open to his eyes."[12] If then, man makes so much of his knowledge that the Apostle says, "knowledge puffs up,"[13] how should he admire the knowledge of God, in comparison with which all knowledge of man is ignorance?

---

[11] Ps. 31 (32):9.
[12] Heb. 4:13.
[13] 1 Cor. 8:1.

Chapter IV
The Soul Has Practical Knowledge of Law; the Highest Law Is in the Mind of God

FOURTHLY, there is another kind of knowledge to be found in the human soul, which does not consist in speculation, but action. This is why there are so many books of philosophers on vices and virtues, so many laws of princes, and counsels of lawyers, to many institutions and exercises to acquire the art of living well. The admirable light of reason is discerned in all these things, in which we are by far superior to the animals. Yet, all of these things are nothing to the eternal law, which is in force in the mind of the Creator, from which like an abundant fount all laws and rights remain. "There is one lawgiver and judge,"[14] as St. James says, namely God. He is the truth, and justice, and wisdom, "through whom kings reign, and the makers of laws decree just things."[15] You will never find out the art of living well until you are admitted into the school of Christ, who is the one and true Master;[16] by his word and example you will learn that justice which abounds more than the justice of the Scribes and Pharisees, I even add that of the philosophers. A justice whose end is "charity from a pure heart and a good conscience and a faith unfeigned."[17]

---

[14] Jas. 4:12.
[15] Prov. 8:15.
[16] Matt. 23:8.
[17] 1 Tim. 1:5.

Chapter V
The Soul of Man Discovers Science; God Is the Fount of Knowledge and Wisdom, Who Invents All Things

FIFTHLY, the soul of man has a third type of knowledge, which consists in ingeniously making things. Now, spiders know how to make their webs, birds their nests, bees their honey, and foxes their holes; but animals do one and the same thing, and in the same manner by an instinct of nature. The human soul, endowed with reason and judgment, devises countless skills whereby it commands and dominates the animals, whether they will to be so dominated or not. Wings are of no use to birds, nor the depths of the sea for fish, nor incredible strength to bears and lions, fierceness to horses and mules, nor speed to stags and goats. For even children capture birds with birdlime and nets, and a man by ingenious craft learned also to surround lions and bears and lock them up in iron cages, catch boars and stags with ropes, or pierce them with spears, to tame horses and mules with a bridle and make them obey his command.

What will I say of the science of sailing? What a great light of brilliance shined on the soul of man when it taught great ships laden with heavy burdens not only to run with oars as if they were feet, but even to fly with sails as though they were wings! Who is not astounded by the cleverness of man, if he were to observe the farms, vineyards, orchards, gardens, fish-ponds, the different channels of waters to irrigate gardens, and lead in to make the land arable? What about architecture? Who does not marvel at the palaces, Churches, cities, castles, towers, amphitheaters, pyramids, and obelisks? I will omit the arts of painting and sculpture, whereby the faces of men and other things are so lively expressed in color and marble, that sometimes they are taken to be real, and not as painted or sculpted. I will say nothing of other arts devised by man for necessity, profit, or pleasure, for they are so many that they can hardly be numbered.

Well now, my soul, give thanks to God, since it has pleased him to make your nature so different from the natures of other living creatures; lift up the eyes of your mind to your Creator, in whom there is the true fount of that genius and wisdom which created all things. From that fount all genius flows which is derived unto your nature, and if you admire man's genius because it has learned how to tame wild beasts by skill and craft, admire God's welcome so much the more, who is served and obeyed not merely by living things, and even inanimate creation. And if it seems like a great thing to you that man has invented the science of sailing on the sea, tilling the fields and building houses, how much more let it seem to you that God has built the heavens, the earth, and the sea, and all things which are in them. Lastly, if you marvel at the lively painting on canvas, or the sculpting of the face of man from marble as though he were alive, why don't you marvel at the skill of your Creator, who made a true living man from the mud, and a true living woman from his rib? Add, that man can do nothing without God, but God does all things by himself without anyone's help.

Chapter VI
Man's Free Will Compared with the Freedom of God

SIXTHLY, the human soul has been endowed with freedom of the will, which it has in common with God himself and the angels, whereby he especially stands apart from all other created things. This is a great nobility, and an admirable excellence. Yet, freedom is so much greater in God, the creator of all things, that the freedom of the soul seems to be hardly more than a shadow in comparison. First, the freedom of the human will is weak, and prone to choose easy things which are evil and harmful. The freedom of God's will is the strongest, and can never fail or be inclined to evil. In this way, to die is a weakness of a mortal body, while not being able to die is a property of a glorified body; so also to be able to sin is a weakness of free will, not to be able to sin will be a property of the same will when God has conferred this by grace in the heavenly homeland, which he always possesses by nature. Next, our free will is indeed free, to be able to will and not will, and actually will and not will, but it does not have the ability to effect what it wills, or that what it refuses would not come into being, even in himself; how much more in others? Listen to the Apostle lamenting in his epistle to the Romans, "Not the good which I will, but the evil which I hate, that I do."[18] And who among us does not experience this? I will to pray attentively to God, and I command my imagination not to wander about and cause me to think of other things while I pray; and yet, I cannot keep to my duty; rather, when I am less careful about this, I find myself deluded by it, and interrupting my prayer while lost in other thoughts. I do not will inordinate desire or to be angry apart from the order of reason, and by free will I command my irascible and concupiscible appetites which are in me, which should be obedient to right reason, and not be seduced by the bodily senses; and yet reason is not obeyed, nor that done which I would, but that which I would not. What is altogether admirable and miserable is the soul commands the body, and is immediately obeyed; the soul commands itself, and it is resisted! As St. Augustine says, "What is this unnatural thing? The mind commands

---

[18] Rom. 7:15.

the hand to move, and it does it with such speed that the command is hardly discerned from the execution of it, and the mind is the mind, and the hand a body! The mind commands the mind to be willing, and it is the same thing and yet it does not do it... But it does not will it fully, and therefore, it does not fully command. Consequently it is no strange thing, but a weakness of the mind, which does not fully rise, being lifted up by truth and weighed down by habit."[19] On the other hand, the free will of God is joined with absolute power, as it is written: "He has done everything that he wills;"[20] and, "There is no one that can resist your will."[21]

This is why, My soul, if you are wise, do not boast of the force of your free will until you come into the freedom of the glory of the sons of God,[22] where your heavenly physician will cure all of your ills, and fill your desire with all good. In the meantime, weep daily, and say to God with the prophet, "Be my helper, do not forsake me."[23] And seven times a day, do not repeat out of habit, rather, with attention and from the heart, "O God, come to my assistance; Lord, make haste to help me."[24]

CHAPTER VII
The Rational Will of the Soul Has Power to Desire Spiritual Goods; God Is Himself the Highest Good, Which Is Charity

SEVENTHLY, the human soul has a rational will, which not

---

[19] *Confess.* 8,9.
[20] Ps. 113 (114):9.
[21] Esth. 13:9.
[22] Rom. 8:21.
[23] Ps. 26 (27):9.
[24] Ps. 69 (70):2.

only has the power to desire the present, particular and corporeal good, for such things appeal to the animals, but also absent, general and spiritual goods, which are shown by faith or reason and truly the infinite and supreme good, which is God. Moreover, this is what causes a man to have the capacity for great virtues, and especially charity, the queen of all virtues. Brute animals love, but with the love of concupiscence; they are altogether unaware of the love of friendship. Now my soul, you have been made capable of that gift by God, which is the fount of all gifts and that which so joins with God the supreme good, that he shall remain in you, and you in him, namely the fount of that luminous and beautiful charity. "For God is charity, and he that abides in charity abides in God, and God in him."[25]

Now, if the happiness of a created will is so great, what are we to think of the happiness with which the uncreated will is fulfilled? Only the will of God is capable of infinite love, with which the infinite goodness of God is worthy to the loved. His will does not lack virtues, or need to be directed by his understanding, since they are all one seeing that wisdom and charity in God is the same thing.

Chapter VIII

The Presence of the Soul in the Body is a Mirror of the Existence of God in Created Things

EIGHTHLY, the human soul is in the human body, but far otherwise than the souls of animals in their bodies. The souls of animals are material, and extended according to their bodies; so that a part of it is in a part of their body, and the whole in their whole body. Yet the human soul, because

---

[25] 1 Jn. 4:16.

The Eighth Step: The Rational Soul

it is an indivisible spirit, is after an admirable manner whole in all, and whole in every part; so that, although it fills the whole body, at the same time, it occupies no place in the body; and when the body grows, the soul does not grow, rather it begins to be where before it was not. Now, if a limb is cut away or withered, the soul is not diminished or withered, rather, it ceases to be in that limb where previously it was, without any harm or mutilation. This is a true mirror of the existence of God in created things. God is an indivisible spirit, and still he fills the whole world, and all its parts, and when any creature is produced, God begins to be in it, and yet he is not moved. Now, when any creature is perhaps destroyed, or dies, God is not destroyed, nor dies, rather, he ceases to be in it, nevertheless, he does not change places. As a result, God and the soul are the same in these matters. Nevertheless, in many matters, as is proper, God excels; accordingly, to be in the body and rule it, as well as move it, the soul must become the form of the body, and be joined with it in such a way that the soul and body becomes one man. Yet God does not need to become the form or soul of the world, nor is one substance made from him and the world. Rather, his immensity is such that he is everywhere, his indivisible unity such that he is completely everywhere, and his omnipotence such that he rules all things, carries all things, and moves all things. Next, although the soul is said to exist in the whole body, nevertheless, it is not properly in the living parts, hence it is not in the humors, the hairs, the fingernails, or in the dried and dead members.

God is in all things both corporeal and spiritual without exception; nor can it happen that anything would exist wherein God is not present. The soul is also only in her own body, which is narrow and straight, and where all the parts are continued together. God, however, is in this universality of things, although it is very great and the parts of it are not continued together, but contiguous and united. Now, if more worlds were made God would be in them all, since it is written, "The heaven and the Heaven of Heavens do not contain you."[26] Even if new heavens and earths were multiplied without end, God would fill them all, for no place can exist where he is not.

Chapter IX
The Soul Is in Some Sense an Image of the Most Holy Trinity

NINTHLY, the human soul, apart from those things which have been said, also has an image in itself of the most holy Trinity, although it is obscure. Not only because it has the power to remember, the force to understand and the force to love, but also because its mind, by its understanding, forms its own word, and love proceeds from the mind and the word, because that which is known and represented by the word as good is thus loved and desired by the will. Nevertheless, God the Father begot God the Word in a higher and more divine fashion, and the Father as well as the word breathed out God the Holy Spirit, the living fount of all chaste love. As a result, the mystery of the Trinity surpasses all natural knowledge, nor can a philosopher attain to it without supernatural light, no matter how learned he may be. Accordingly, the soul of man produces a word, and love, which are not substances, but accidents, and thereby are not persons. God the Father, on the other hand, begot the Word unto himself and the Father as well as the Word breathed out the Holy Spirit consubstantial to them both. Thus, the Father, the Son, and the Holy Spirit are truly three persons. The human soul also produces a word which does not remain long, and the will produces a love which

---

[26] 2 Chron. 6:18.

does not last long, but God the Father did beget the eternal Word, and the Father and the Word did breathe out the eternal Holy Spirit. God cannot be without his Word and Spirit. Moreover, the human soul, by one word represents only one thing; and therefore, it multiplies the words not only of the mind, but also of the mouth. The human will likewise must produce many acts of love, if it will love many things; but God with one Word speaks all truth, and with one act of love loves all good things.

Chapter X
The Soul Bestows Natural Things on the Body; God Bestows Heavenly Gifts upon the Soul

TENTHLY and lastly, the soul of man, so long as it is in the body it is not seen, heard, moved, nor hardly conceived to be there. Just the same, all good things are derived from it to the body, as sense, motion, speech, subsistence, beauty, strength, and the like. Now, how could a man see, hear, speak, walk, subsist, and be strong, beautiful, amiable, except that his soul were in him? Why would he not see, hear, speak, and move but lies disfigured, useless and unseen, except that his soul had departed, from where these benefits proceeded? In this way your God, my soul, while he lives in you by his grace, causes you to see what he spoke in you, so that you would walk in the way of the commandments towards the heavenly Jerusalem, and speak in prayer to God and in good exhortation to your neighbor, and subsist persevering in good works, and be strong in the battle line against your invisible enemies, becoming beautiful in the eyes of the invisible God and his angels.

Now take heed lest God's grace would depart from you, which is the life of your soul, and you fall into the losses of the first death, and thereby be carried to the second death, from which there is no resurrection. Oh, if the Lord would open the eyes of your mind, so you would behold the beauty of a soul that is united to him in charity! What a place he prepares for it! What joys he promises it! How lovingly he looks upon it! With what longing it is awaited by the angels and souls of the blessed! Then would you not endure that so great a beauty should be blemished with the least spot, and if it were to happen, you would endeavor to wash it away with floods of tears. This is what St. Francis did, as St. Bonaventure relates, although he could not follow the immaculate Lamb without some spot, he endeavored just the same to cleanse his soul with daily showers of tears from all spots of offenses.[27] Now, if only God would open your interior eyes! Then you might see how filthy the soul of a sinner really is, how it smells as foul as a rotten corpse, and how God and his angels refuse to look at it, even if it happens to dwell in a beautiful body which is pleasing to the eyes of men. Truly, you would be so terrified that you would never for any reason allow yourself to become like it, or to remain in that state for long.

---

[27] *Vita S. Francesci* 5,7.

THE NINTH STEP
From The Consideration of the Angels

CHAPTER I
An Angel Is Altogether a Perfect Spirit and a Created One; God, However, Is Uncreated and Absolutely Perfect

WE HAVE now come to the highest step of the climb to God upon the ladder which we have constructed from created substances, since if we are speaking only of natural perfection, there is no created substance more sublime than the angelic. First, we will consider the angels according to the excellence of their nature; secondly, according to the sublimity of their grace, and lastly, according to the duties that they perform. It is not our intention to take on a full disputation regarding angels, but only to touch upon such things as will help us to elevate our minds to God.

Now, if an angel is compared with man's rational soul, it may appropriately be described as a perfect soul, even as the soul of man may be described as an imperfect angel. The prophet speaks in this way by reason of his soul, when he says, "You have made him a little less than the angels."[1] An angel is a perfect spiritual substance; the soul an imperfect spiritual substance because it is the form of the body and but one part of man. As a result, an angel is all spirit; man partly spirit and partly flesh, or, partly an angel and partly an animal. In other words, an angel is all gold, man partly gold

---
[1] Ps. 8:6.

and partly clay. So truly then the prophet said that man was made a little less than the angels. Now, it is also true that the human soul, because it is a part of man, is little less than an angel. This is why it follows that an angel is more like to God than a man or his soul, for God is a spirit, and not a body or form of a body.

Notwithstanding this similarity of an angel to God, God is a spirit infinitely excelling the dignity of an angel; for God is a spirit uncreated, eternal, immense, alone almighty, alone good, alone wise, alone the most high. If then, my soul, you will confess that you admire the nature of angels (with reason), how much more should you admire and reverence the nature of God, who excels them without all comparison!

Chapter II
Of the Understanding and Knowledge of Angels

IT IS not only by nature that an angel may be described as a perfect man, and a man an imperfect angel, but also by knowledge and understanding. Man, because he must use the ministry of his senses and examines from effects to causes, and from causes to effects, understands with labor, and little by little acquires knowledge for himself, this is why sometimes doubt takes hold, sometimes he is wretchedly deceived, and rarely does he arrive at certain understanding. An angel, on the other hand, considers a thing with a unique gaze, and discerns cause and effect at once; not only does he penetrate the accidents, but even the very substance of a thing, and he not only sees corporeal things, but also spiritual ones.

Now man, while he is a pilgrim on earth, in regard to matters pertaining to understanding, is not a little less than the Angels, but much less. Even though he excels in skill and

The Ninth Step: A Consideration of the Angels

study of philosophy, yet in comparison with an angel he may truly be considered a child or a infant. The prophet was not wrong when he sang of us mortals, "From the mouth of infants and sucklings you have perfected praise."[2] Listen to Solomon, the wisest of men, and his judgment of our knowledge, whereby we are so puffed up, "All things are difficult, man cannot explain them in a word,"[3] and, "He has delivered the world to their consideration, so that man cannot find out the work which God has made from the beginning to the end."[4] If all things then are difficult, and such as man cannot explain, and if man understands nothing in the visible world, from the first creature to the last, I say nothing so perfectly as that he is able to explain the nature, properties, accidents, powers and the rest of the things hidden in it, how great are the errors that will he fall into if he undertakes to search out the things which are above heaven?

This is why if you are wise, O my soul, follow the knowledge of salvation and wisdom of the saints, which consists in fear of God and keeping his commandments; delight more in prayer than in disputation, edifying charity more than proud knowledge; for this is the path which leads to life and the kingdom of heaven, where the equality of the angels, who always see the face of the Father who is in heaven, will at last be given to us little ones.

---

[2] Ps. 8:3.
[3] Eccl. 1:8.
[4] Eccl. 3:2.

CHAPTER III
The Dominion of the Angels Over Bodies; and the Almighty Creator

THERE is also a third thing in which the human soul is not only made a little less, but much less than an angel, namely, the power and command over bodies. Man's soul moves the body by the command of the will, but it cannot move other bodies in this way; and it moves the body by progressive motion upon the earth, but cannot suspend it upon the water, elevate it above the air, or carry it wherever it wills. Angels, however, can do all of these things by the force of the spirit and command of the will. In this way, an angel took up Habakkuk, and in short order carried him to Babylon to bring Daniel his dinner, and then carried him back to Palestine.[5] A man also cannot fight in spirit alone with his hands and weapons; but an angel, by the power of spirit without hands or weapons, can encounter and overcome a whole army of men. In this way an angel slew one hundred eighty-five thousand Assyrians on the spot.[6]

Now, if angels can do these things, what can their Lord and Creator do? He truly made all things from nothing, and can reduce all things to nothing. Furthermore, the human soul can make things by painting, and with industry and labor make the image of a man seem so alive that it almost lives and breathes; but an angel can, without labor of hands or instruments, almost in an instant, adapt a body of this sort from the elements in such a way, that prudent men will regard it as a human body because it walks, speaks, eats, drinks, can be touched, and even washed. In this way

---

[5] Dan. 14:32 *et seqq.*
[6] 4 King. 19:35.

Abraham prepared food for the angels and washed their feet,[7] as the Apostle explains, he received angels as guests thinking they had been men.[8] The same thing also happened to his nephew Lot, when he received two angels as strangers in his house.[9] The angel Raphael remained with young Tobit in a similar manner, walking, speaking, eating, and drinking for many days, as if he had been a man indeed; but notwithstanding departing after, he said, "I seemed to eat with you, and to drink, but I use an invisible food and drink," and suddenly, "he vanished from their sight."[10] Surely, it is admirable, and proceeds from great power, to so frame a body on the spot to that it appears to have no difference from a living body of a man, and again, at his pleasure, suddenly to dissolve the same body so that no vestige remains. If then, the power of angels is so great, how great is the power of the Creator of angels who gave them that power! Truly, as the knowledge of angels and men is ignorance in comparison with the knowledge of God, and as the justice of angels and men is injustice in comparison with the justice of God, so all the power of angels and men is weakness in comparison with the power of God. Therefore, it is truly said that our God alone is wise,[11] alone good,[12] and alone powerful.[13]

---

[7] Gen. 13:2 *et seqq.*
[8] Heb. 13:2.
[9] Gen. 19:1, *seqq.*
[10] Tob. 12:19, 21.
[11] Rom. 16:27.
[12] Lk. 18:19.
[13] 1 Tim. 6:15.

CHAPTER IV
The Place and Motion of Angels, and the Omnipresence of God

LASTLY, if we consider the place of angels and men, we will find a human soul in that respect also, he is not a little less than the angels, but altogether much less (I gladly use the word which the Apostle uses in Heb. 2:7). For God has appointed a place on earth for the human soul, and in heaven, namely, in his palace, a place for angels. "For the heaven of heavens belongs to our Lord; but the earth he has given to the children of men."[14]

This is why our Lord calls them "the angels of heaven,"[15] and also says, "There will be joy in heaven upon one sinner that does penance.... There shall be joy before the angels of God over one sinner that does penance."[16] Besides, God has bound the soul to the body in such a way, that it cannot move from place to place without it; but the angels are not bound to any body, rather, they have been given the power to pass from heaven to earth, and from earth to heaven, or wherever they wish to go, with incredible speed. In this way an angel by the dignity of its nature is near to God, and in their fleetness imitate God's omnipotence as much as they can. God is everywhere by the immensity of nature, and as a result, does not need to change his place; angels, by the swiftness of their motion pass so quickly from place to place and so demonstrate their presence in every place that they seem after a fashion to be everywhere.

Now, my soul, if you will listen to the Lord of angels, there is no reason why you would envy the high place which the angels have, as well as their tireless motion. For

---

[14] Ps. 113 (114):24.
[15] Matt. 24:36.
[16] Lk. 15:7, 10.

The Ninth Step: A Consideration of the Angels 125

not only will you be equal to the angels when you are freed from the body, but when you return to your body, which Christ will conform to the body of his glory,[17] you will possess heaven as your own house with that body, and after it has become spiritual,[18] it will immediately be in that place which you, its soul, will and command it without effort or weariness. Your Lord does not deceive you, when he says in the Gospel, "In my Father's house there are many mansions, ... I go and prepare a place for you, ... If I go and prepare a place for you, I come again, and will take you to myself, so that where I am, you also will be.[19] Father, I will that where I am, they also may be with me, and that they may see my glory which you have given me."[20] Now, you are not ignorant of where Christ is, and what body he has. You confess it every day, when you say, "On the third day he rose again from the dead; he ascended into heaven." And you also know that his body, after the resurrection, sometimes entered among his disciples, although the doors were shut;[21] and he departed from them, not walking but vanishing, namely, he transferred his body from them so quickly that it seemed as though he had been a spirit and not a body.[22] Yet, if you seek after his glory, you must first configure your body to the body of humiliation of Christ, and then Christ will configure your body to the body of his glory.[23] "For Christ suffered for us, leaving us an example so that we may follow his steps."[24] What are his steps? "Who committed no sin, nor was guile found in his mouth, who when he was reviled, did not revile, when he suffered, he did

---

[17] Phil. 3:21.
[18] 1 Cor. 15:44.
[19] John 14:2, 3.
[20] John 17:24.
[21] Lk. 24:31.
[22] Jn. 20:19.
[23] Phil. 3:21.
[24] 1 Pet. 2:21-23.

not threaten."²⁵ There are two steps of Christ, which if you do not tread, you will lose your way to heaven: Firstly, you must not do evil, but suffer it, and there it follows to do good, and not expect good in return. Or, which is the sum of all, to love your neighbor for God's sake, with a true and pure love of friendship, not of lust, or favor, not on account of a human reward, but being content with God's reward, which surpasses every measure.

Chapter V
What Sort of Grace is Given to Angels, and What to Men

LET us not come to the dignity of the angels according to grace. Truly man is also diminished more than a little less than the angels in the fact that God created angels in the beginning in such a way that he instantaneously made their nature and infused grace into them, as St. Augustine witnesses.²⁶ Then, as soon as their minds first turned to God they adhered to him by charity, and after the reprobate angels fell, they were crowned with glory and beatitude. Consequently, their pilgrimage was very short, but their house in heaven eternal (if indeed that short period of time between their creation and beatitude may be called a pilgrimage). Now we, in our creation, received grace with our nature in our first parent and not in ourselves; therefore, by his fall we all fell. "In whom all have sinned."²⁷ Although we are reconciled to God by Christ Jesus, the mediator of God and man, nevertheless, we are condemned to continual banishment; and while we are in the body we are pilgrims from our Lord, "For we walk by faith and not by sight," and

---

²⁵ Ibid.
²⁶ *De Civ. Dei* 9, 2.
²⁷ Rom. 5:12.

The Ninth Step: A Consideration of the Angels

it is a great affliction to pious men and such as sigh after heaven, that we are here to live among cruel enemies, where there is danger that being surrounded and taken by them we will at length be excluded from the possession of our sweetest country. Hence these words proceed, "Woe is me that my sojourn is prolonged. I have dwelt with the inhabitants of Cedar, my soul has long been a sojourner."[28] Now, although in this we are less than angels, nevertheless, God's mercy greatly comforts us men for two reasons. One, because he has placed one man and one woman from our race, Christ and Mary, ahead of all the angels in the kingdom of heaven. The second is the fact that many men, although they are inferior in the gifts of nature than all the angels, just the same, he has willed them to be higher than many angels, and even equal to some of the highest by a gift of grace.

Certainly, St. John Chrysostom did not hesitate to place the princes of the Apostles, Peter and Paul, where the seraphim fly and glorify God, which also piously believed about St. John the Baptist, and several others. Moreover, as the good angels entered into glory after their first merit, so the evil angels were condemned to eternal punishment after their first sin. Men should not, therefore, complain of a longer road, since on it they often or even frequently correct their falls, and by penance obtain pardon for their offenses.

---

[28] Ps. 119 (120):5.

CHAPTER VI
The Offices of the Angels Are Considered

NOW it remains for us to speak a little about the offices of the angels, which are five:

1. Always to praise their maker with hymns and songs. Now, that we may understand how much God esteems this ministry, we must consider that the highest angels are appointed for this office, who being, as it were, the first singers in that choir, all the other orders of angels follow with incredible rejoicing. Listen to Isaiah: "I saw the Lord sitting upon a high and lofty throne, and his train filled the temple. Upon it stood the seraphim, the one had six wings, and the other had six wings, with two they covered his face, and with two they covered his feet, and with two they flew. And they cried one to another and said: Holy, holy, holy, the Lord God of hosts, all the earth is full of his glory."[29] Here, you hear the name *seraphim*, which are the chief of the highest order. You see them cover his face and feet in sign of reverence, as if they would not dare to behold his face or touch his bare feet; you see they fly continually while they sing, which signifies their desire to come still nearer to God. These two things are necessary for those who desire to please God while they sing his praises, so that they would join love with reverence and reverence with love. The prophet David declared this, saying, "Serve the Lord in fear and rejoice to him with trembling."[30]

May you learn from this, O my soul, what great veneration God is worthy of, when the supreme princes of heaven, who always assist him, and always see his face, and

---

[29] Isa. 6:1-3.
[30] Ps. 2:11.

do not ever dare to neglect fear and reverence from their high state nor from so long a familiarity, while they sing his praises. Now, dust and ashes, what will you answer when you are convicted in the judgment for the drowsiness and distractions in a work so divine that you were not worthy to be employed in? From now on, learn now that you have been taught by so great an example to praise your God with fear, reverence, attention, vigilance, and love.

2. Another office of the angels is to offer up the prayers of men to God, and to commend them also by their suffrage; for the angel Raphael speaks this way in Tobit: "When you prayed with tears, and buried the dead, and left your dinner, I offered your prayer to the Lord;"[31] and in the Apocalypse, John saw an angel standing before the altar with a golden censer, "And there were given to him many incenses, that he should give of the prayers of all saints upon the altar of gold, which is before the throne of God."[32]

Now, the great mercy of our God also appears in this, for he was not content, first by his prophets and after by his Son and his apostles, to exhort us to pray, but also promised to give whatever we should ask: "Ask and it shall be given to you;"[33] ... "If you will ask my Father anything in my name he will give it to you."[34] Besides this promise, he also added a reward to those who ask, "But you, when you pray, enter into your chamber and after you have shut the door, pray to your Father in secret, and your Father who sees in secret will repay you,"[35] namely, a reward besides the things which you asked for. For so our Lord speaks in that place of prayer and almsgiving, saying, "Your Father who sees in secret will repay you."

---

[31] Tob. 12:12.
[32] Apoc. 8:3.
[33] Lk. 11:9.
[34] Jn. 16:23.
[35] Matt. 6:6.

God is not content with this proof of paternal piety, but has appointed the angels as masters of requests to take charge of the prayers and petitions of the poor, and to present and read them in his sight so that no one of their petitions may be forgotten. What prince in the world ever promised rewards to those that came to demand mercy or justice from him? Nevertheless, those who come to the princes of the world are men, and the princes themselves also are men made from the same mud and subject to the same Prince, almighty God. Now, albeit that it seems much to reward those who ask, nevertheless, should it not seem much to give them free access to appoint faithful masters of requests to keep their petitions, and to offer them up and are eager for their speedy march.

3. The third office of the Angels has been placed in the fact that they are sent as ambassadors to show the things which God means to be shown, and especially those things concerned with the business of redemption and eternal salvation. The Apostle speaks in this way to the Hebrews, "Are not all [angels] ministering spirits sent to minister for them who will receive the inheritance of salvation?"[36]

We also see that everywhere in the Old Testament, angels appeared to the patriarchs and prophets,[37] and revealed to them the things which God commanded them. We also read in the New Testament that the angel Gabriel was sent as an ambassador from God to Zachariah and to the Virgin Mother of God.[38] Angels were also sent to the shepherds,[39] to St. Joseph;[40] and after the resurrection of our Lord, to the women who stayed at the tomb;[41] and after the

---

[36] Heb. 1:14.
[37] Gen. 18:2 *seq.*, 19:1 *seq.*, 22:1; Dan. 9:21 *seq.*, 14:32 *seq.*
[38] Lk. 1:11 *seq.* 1:26 *seq.*
[39] Lk. 2:9 *seq.*
[40] Matt. 1:20 *seq.*, 2:13, 19.
[41] Matt. 28:2 *seq.*; Jn. 20:12 *seq.*

The Ninth Step: A Consideration of the Angels 131

Ascension to all the disciples.[42] Now, if anyone were to ask why God, who is everywhere, and can easily speak by himself in the hearts of men, just the same sends his angels, it seems that the reason is that men may understand that God regards their affairs, and that he governs and orders all things. Otherwise, they might persuade themselves that God's inspiration proceeds from their own discourse and counsel. Now, when they see or hear that angels are sent by God, and the things which the angels foretell truly come to pass, they cannot doubt that God foresees man's affairs, and chiefly directs and dispose such things as pertain to the salvation of his elect.

4. The fourth office of the angels is to protect men both in particular and in general. It pleased the goodness of God to commend weak mortals into the protection of his most powerful servants, and to appoint them just like tutors over children, guardians over infants, patrons over clients, shepherds over sheep, physicians over sick folks, defenders over orphans and such as cannot defend themselves but under the wings of the mightier.

David witnesses the protection of men in particular, "He has given his angels charge of you, that they would keep you in all your ways."[43] Christ himself is also a faithful witness of this fact, "See to it that you despise not one of these little ones, for I say to you, that their angels in heaven always see the face of my Father which is in heaven."[44] Daniel is also a witness in regard to the protectors of provinces and kingdoms, since he called the angel protector of the kingdom of Persia the king of the Persians, and the protector of the kingdom of the Greeks, the names king of the Greeks, and the protector of the sons of Israel he calls by

---

[42] Act. 1:10-11.
[43] Ps. 90 (91):11.
[44] Matt. 18:10.

his own name, Michael.[45] Lastly, John writes about the protectors of Churches in the Apocalypse, where he mentions the angel of the Church of Ephesus, and the angel of the Church of Smyrna, and of others. Therefore, in every kingdom there are two kings, the one a visible man, the other an invisible angel; and in the universal Catholic Church there are two supreme Pontiffs appointed under Christ our Lord, the one a visible man, the other an invisible angel, which we believe to be St. Michael the Archangel. Just as the synagogue of the Jews in ancient times, so now the Church of the Christians reverences him for its patron.

Don't you see, my soul, how concerned that Majesty, who does not need our goods, is with us his servants? What could he do to show his great love that he has not yet done? He has overwhelmed us with benefits so that we would gladly remain with him; he has he has guarded us with a watch, that we would not escape him, and he has surrounded us with protectors lest we would be carried off. What would he do, if we were his treasure, as indeed he is our only treasure?

Therefore, my soul, yield at last to his love, and when you have been overcome by such love, surrender, deliver, give your whole self, leaving no part behind, to his service and will by an irrevocable oath and vow: do not allow yourself to be moved by anything which is seen, rather, think of invisible things, and sigh after them. "For the things that are seen are temporal, but those which are not seen are eternal."[46]

5. The last office of the Angels is that they are also armed soldiers or generals, to bring vengeance upon the gentiles, and correction among the people. It was angels who burned notorious cities with fire and sulphur,[47] who

---

[45] Dan. 10:5 *seqq*.
[46] 2 Cor. 4:18.
[47] Gen. 19:13 *seq*.

killed the firstborn of all Egypt;[48] which in one attack destroyed many thousand Assyrians;[49] and they shall be angels which, on the last day, will separate the wicked from the midst of the just, and "will cast them into the furnace of fire."[50]

So, let good men love the holy angels as their countrymen, and let wicked men dread their power, which are the executioners of Almighty God's wrath from whose hands no one will be able to deliver them.

---

[48] Exod. 12:12, *seq.*
[49] 4 Kings 19:35.
[50] Matt. 13:49-50.

THE TENTH STEP
From the Consideration of God's Essence, by the Similarity of a Corporeal Mass

CHAPTER I
A General Consideration of the Greatness of God from the Four Dimensions of Corporeal Things

E have ascended as much as we could by created substances, nevertheless we have not yet obtained the very notice of God, to which can be obtained by observation even in this valley of tears. It remains, therefore, to see whether by the dimensions of a corporeal quantity which we know, we might go up the breadth, length, height, and depth of God's invisible essence. Now, among created things they are said to be great which have found great dimensions. And God in the Psalms, and in many other places, is called great, and his greatness without end."[1] Truly St. Bernard, a man excellent in contemplation, in his books *On Consideration* which he wrote to Pope Eugene III, framed from these dimensions certain steps to know God. Yet, he was not the first inventor of a ladder of this sort, rather, he learned this manner of ascent from the Apostle who was rapt into the Third Heaven and entered paradise, learned this manner of ascent, since he says in his epistle to the Ephesians, "That you might be able to understand with all the saints what is

---

[1] Ps. 44 (45):3.

the breadth and length and height as well as depth."[2] If anyone would consider with attention, he will certainly find that there is nothing full and lasting outside of God, rather all is small, short, empty, and superficial; in God, however, immensity is true breadth, eternity is true length, omnipotence is true height, and incomprehensibility is true depth."[3]

If someone were to consider the matter attentively, he will certainly find that there is nothing without God which is full and solid, but all things are small, short, lowly, empty, or superficial. Now, in God his immensity is true breadth, his eternity is true length, his omnipotence is true height, and his incomprehensibility is true depth. It is not enough to lightly touch upon these considerations if someone means to go up and find what he seeks; rather, it behooves us to fully understand them, as we already quoted from the Apostle, "That you may be able to comprehend with all the saints what is the breadth and length and height and depth." He truly comprehends who, while thinking very attentively is altogether persuaded the matter is so, and being persuaded in such a way that after he has sold everything, he will hasten to buy the treasure he has found, and so the Apostle adds, "with all the saints." In fact, the saints alone fully understand, and no man understands as he ought unless he will first become a saint.

Now, St. Augustine does not oppose what we have said, when in his Epistle to Honoratus he writes that the Apostle describes the Cross of Christ by its breadth, length, height, and depth;[4] namely the breadth of the Cross was where his hands were nailed, the length to which his body cleaved; the height where his title was written, and the depth was fastened and hid in the earth. I say that St. Augustine does

---

[2] Eph. 3:15.
[3] Eph. 3:18.
[4] *Epist.* 140, 26, n. 64.

not oppose our purpose, rather more he confirms it; for the Cross of Christ is the way to obtain true breadth, length, height, and depth. Although to the eyes of men the Cross seems small, short, degraded, and of no depth, yet the arms of it have been extended from East to West, and from North to South, i.e. the glory of it has reached up to the highest heaven, which, after the manner of a key, it has opened for the elect; and has pierced to the lowest hell, which it has closed from the same elect forever.

Chapter II
The Broadness of the Essence of God Is His Immeasurable Goodness

LET us begin from the essence, then proceed to the attributes. The essence of God may be described as the broadest in many ways. First in itself, because it is truly infinite, and embraces all the perfections of created things, which are, or may be, without end. Whatsoever exists, will exist, or may exist, is without a doubt contained in God in the most eminent manner. Thus, created things are good with an addition, as a good man, a good horse, a good house, a good garment, and similar things; but God is all good. For when Moses said, "Show me your glory," God answered, "I will show you all good."[5]

If anyone were to have a thing with him that contained all the objects of the senses in the highest perfection, so that he would never willingly leave home to see something, or hear something, or smell, or taste, or touch, since he had at home as many delights in that one thing as any sensual man could desire: would not that thing be very precious?

---

[5] Exod. 33:18-19.

Moreover, if that thing were to contain as much of an abundance of every kind of riches as a man greedy beyond measure could desire, so that he would not wish to leave home to acquire anything further, wouldn't that be more precious and beloved? And again, if that thing could furnish honors and dignities to its possessor, so many more than the most ambitious man could conceive of, wouldn't it seem to surpass all notion of price? And if that thing not only satisfied the desires of men, but even angels (the greater they are, the more things they know than men), what would you say then? Yet, notwithstanding the goodness of that thing would be far inferior to the goodness of God, which is so great that it suffices to satisfy the infinite desire, or rather infinite capacity of God. O admirable breadth of perfection of the essence of God, which embraces such an immense goodness that it wholly suffices for his infinite capacity, for God never goes out of himself, because he has every good thing within himself. Before the world was made he was as rich and as happy as he was afterward, because nothing was made by God which did not always exist in God in a higher manner.

Do you understand, O my soul, what happiness that you will enjoy in heaven if you love God on earth? What happiness you will lose if you do not love him? Then God will give himself, namely, every good to those who love him, when he will say: "Good and faithful servant, enter into the joy of your Lord."[6]

---

[6] Matt. 25:21.

CHAPTER III
The Breadth of the Essence of God Is His Immeasurable Goodness

NEXT, God is immense in another way, because he altogether fills all things which are in created things. "I fill heaven and earth, says the Lord."[7] And if there were more worlds he would fill them all. "If I will ascend into heaven, you are there, if I will descend into hell, you are there." I also add, were I to go to heaven or under heaven or out of heaven, I will not be alone, because you are there; nor can I be anywhere but in You, and by You, which carries all things by the word of your power.[8] Furthermore, God, by his immensity, not only fills all bodies, but also all spirits; for how else could he search the heart unless he were in it? And how could he hear the prayers of the heart unless he gave ear to them? And how could the prophet say, "I will hear what the Lord God will speak to me,"[9] unless God put his mouth to the hears of the heart? Happy is that soul which loves God, because he always has his beloved with him, and cherishes him in his bosom, and is cherished in his bosom, "He that abides in charity, abides in God and God in him."[10]

God does not merely fill all things with his presence, but also with his glory. The seraphim cry out, "That the earth is full of his glory,"[11] and David adds, "O Lord, our Lord, how marvelous is your name in all the earth! Because your magnificence is lifted above the heavens,"[12] in other words:

---

[7] Jer. 23:24.
[8] Heb. 1:3.
[9] Ps. 84 (85):9.
[10] 1 Jn. 4:16.
[11] Isa. 6:3.
[12] Ps. 8:2.

Your name, fame, and glory have not only filled all the earth with admiration, but also ascended and are elevated above the heavens. Sirach says the same, "The work of the Lord is full of his glory."[13] There is no creature in heaven or on earth that does not continually praise God. This is why David in the Psalms,[14] as well as the three children in Daniel,[15] invite all creatures to praise and magnify their Creator, albeit they were not unaware that many creatures were of such a nature that they could not hear what they said; rather, because they knew that all of God's works were good, and so with their beauty, praised their Creator, they rejoiced in them, and exhorted them to do as they did.

Now truly, whosoever has inner eyes will see that all of God's works are as thuribles sending up an odor of the sweetness of his glory. If a man has inner ears, he will hear them like a whole concert of every sort of musical instrument praising God, and saying, "he made us, and not ourselves."[16] Although there is no shortage of wicked men who curse God and blaspheme his name, nevertheless, they are also compelled, even against their will, to praise God just as a work praises a workman; likewise God's power, whereby he made them, his goodness whereby he preserves them, his mercy, whereby he awaits and invites them to repentance, and his justice, whereby he condemns them to punishment, marvelously appear in them. There are many in the world who do not hear these voices of creatures, although they cry without ceasing, but there are innumerable angels and holy men that hear them, and are delighted by them, and they also continually praise their Creator with hymns and canticles.

---

[13] Sirach 42:16.
[14] Ps. 148:1 *seqq.*
[15] Dan. 3:41 *seqq.*
[16] Ps. 99 (100):3.

Chapter IV
The Length of the Divine Essence Is His Eternity

MOREOVER, the length of the divine essence is its eternity, which neither has beginning of duration, nor does it ever end, and it will always consist without any change. "You are the self-same, and your years will not fail."[17] Likewise, Tobit, and after him the Apostle, call God "The King of worlds,"[18] because he alone existed before all worlds and is not subject to worlds, rather he rules and governs them. Other things have beginning and end, and never continue in the same state (or else they have beginning without end or change of substance); yet if their Maker pleases, they will cease to be. So Eternity is proper to God alone, and there was never any prince so proud that among his many other titles he arrogated to himself the title of "eternal", except perhaps, in another sense, as Constantius, who was called eternal Emperor, because he was not Emperor for a certain time, but for a life term.

No you, O my soul, may be numbered among both kinds of creation, for you have a body which began to exist when it was conceived, and by degrees it was born and then grew to that stature which God appointed. Then it began to diminish, and shortly by death it will cease to be. As a result, it never wholly continues in the same state, but is subject to change at every moment. The prophet spoke of your body by comparing it to grass: "In the morning it shall pass like grass, in the morning he will flourish and pass; in the evening it shall fall, harden and be withered."[19] Accordingly in the morning, namely in youth, the body is full of vigor

---

[17] Ps. 101 (102):28.
[18] Tob. 13:6.
[19] Ps. 89 (90):6.

like the grass; then youth follows; at the noontime of youth it flourishes, and soon after old age follows; in the evening of old age it falls by death, and in the grave it is hardened, withered, and turned to dust.

Behold, O my soul, how far your body is from eternity; but you were created in time, whereas before you were nothing, and therein are very unlike your eternal Creator; but being created, your duration is endless, wherein you resemble your Creator. Now, since you are in the body you often change from vice to virtue and from virtue to vice, and according to the state in which you will be found at your exit from the body, you will be judged either to reign forever with God, or forever to be tormented by the devil, so you can make no greater provision than to flee vice and embrace virtue. Therefore, beware, lest you be seduced by the allurements of your flesh, to the everlasting loss both of you and your flesh; rather, crucify it with its vices and concupiscences, so that a little later not only will you live happy forever, but even your flesh will rise again in glory, and remain united with you in the eternity of your God.

Now, although the holy angels and souls of the saints are to become partakers of eternity in that high and happy union with God, by his beatifying vision and love. Such a union will not only have no end, but will also be stable and immovable; nevertheless, they will be able to change and vary their thoughts, affections, and places in different ways; therefore, they will always reverently admire God's eternity above them, in whom there can be no change of thought, affection, or place; for he lacks nothing, rather, has all things present which in eternity of time he might have procured by different changes. Consequently, eternity is a length without end, no less proper to God than the breadth of his immensity.

Chapter V
The Height of God Shows the Nobility of the Divine Nature, Which Is the First Effective and Most High Cause and the Final Example of All Things

IT FOLLOWS that the height of God must be considered according to which it is said to him, "You are the most high."[20] God is the most high by the excellence of nature. Other things are the higher and excellent, the purer they are and more removed from matter. First of all, this is clear in corporeal things. Water is higher than earth because it is purer, and for the same reason air is higher than water, and fire than air, and heaven than fire. Next, we see the same in spiritual things, for the understanding is higher than the sense because the sense has a corporeal organ, which the understanding does not require; likewise, the angelic intellect is higher than the human, because the human intellect requires the aid of the imagination and phantasms, which the angels do not need. Among the angels also, they are the highest which understand more by fewer forms. So God, who alone is pure act, does not need an organ or imagination, or a species, and not even the presence of some object outside of himself, rather, his very essence is all things to it, and it can have nothing which it does not always have in act, and the very thing it has in act, is always a pure and simple act; therefore his nature is the highest and most sublime, nor can it have an equal in any manner. For this reason, he that said, "I will be like unto the most high," was suddenly cast down from heaven into the lowest hell, as Isaiah describes.[21] Christ our Lord also says of him, "I saw

---

[20] Ps. 82 (83):19.
[21] Isa. 14:14.

Satan fall like lightning from heaven."[22]

God is also most high in another manner, because he is the first and highest cause of all things, efficient, exemplar, and final. He is the highest efficient cause, since there is no creature that has any working virtue except from God; but God does not receive from any other. Again, there is no cause which can exercise its own force unless it is moved by God; God, however, is moved by none. Then, the other higher causes in created things are said to be those which are universals, upon which particulars depend, such as heaven, and the angels who move the heavens; God, however, made both the heavens and the angels, consequently he alone is the first and highest efficient cause. Likewise, he is the first exemplary cause, because God made all things according to forms, or ideas, which are contained in himself. Lastly, he is the first final cause, namely, he created all things to reveal his glory, as holy wisdom says in Proverbs.[23] But it is most properly said, that God is also most high because he sits on the highest throne. Isaiah, says, "I saw the Lord sitting upon a high and lofty throne."[24] Then, because a seat has two uses, one to judge and the other to rest, we shall consider each separately.

Chapter VI
God Has a Lofty Throne, for He Is the Highest King and Judge, Bringing Grace to the Humble

FIRST, God has the highest seat because he is the supreme judge. Abraham says to God, "You shall judge all the

---

[22] Lk. 10:18.
[23] Prov. 16:4.
[24] Isa. 6:1.

The Tenth Step: A Consideration of God's Essence

earth,"[25] and David, "God judges gods,"[26] i.e., God judges the judges themselves, who are called gods in the Scriptures. Furthermore, James clearly says, "There is one lawmaker and judge,"[27] that is to say, God alone is the true lawgiver and judge; for he alone gives laws to all and receives them from no one; he judges all and is judged by no one. Then God is not only a judge, but also a king, and so he judges not like a judge appointed by a king, but as the highest commanding king, for which reason he is called "King of kings,"[28] and "great king over all the gods,"[29] and "terrible to the kings of the earth,"[30] because he transfers kingdoms and empires from one nation to another, and takes away the spirit of princes when he pleases. Nor is God only the highest king and judge, but also an absolute Lord, which is the greatest title of all. Kings are not absolute masters over their subjects in such a way that they may, when they please, deprive them of their goods and lives. King Achab may be a witness of this fact, who would have had Naboth's vineyard, yet could not except through the treachery and calumny of his wife, for which reason they both miserably perished. God, however, is truly and properly Lord, and all things serve him, and he serves no one, and he could, at his pleasure, reduce all things to nothing because he made them all from nothing.

Think about it, my soul, what fear and reverence we worms of the earth owe to him that sits upon the highest throne! "If I be the Lord, where is my fear?"[31] If the highest angels of heaven serve him with fear and trembling, what should we weak mortal men do, who dwell on earth with

---

[25] Gen. 18:25.
[26] Ps. 81 (82):1.
[27] Jas. 4:12.
[28] Apoc. 19:16.
[29] Ps. 94 (95):3.
[30] Ps. 75 (76):13.
[31] Mal. 1:6.

the beasts? Now, to some it may seem strange why God, who is the most high, does not love creatures which resemble him, namely, the high and lofty, but the humble and poor. God speaks to Isaiah this way, "Whom shall I look to except the poor little one, and the contrite of spirit, and him that trembles at my words?"[32] David adds, "Our Lord is high and beholds the low things."[33] Truly, God loves high and lofty creatures if therein they resemble him; but then they must be high in deed and not in appearance. God, therefore, does not love the proud which are inflated and puffed up; not truly high. Rather, he loves the humble and those who tremble at his words, and exalts them, and they are high indeed whom he exalts. So those who are humble are high, namely humble in their own eyes, and high in the eyes of God.

If a man had seen not only with his bodily eyes but also with the eyes of his heart, illuminated by God, the rich glutton clothed in fine clothes and purple sitting at his table furnished with all kinds of exquisite food, attended upon by many servants diligently conducting their office, and at the same time, had in like manner beheld poor Lazarus, half-naked and covered with sores, sitting at the rich man's door, and begging to be filled with the crumbs that fell from his table; he would truly have seen the rich man whom the world accounted most happy, to be in the eyes of God and his angels as vile and abominable as the mud and dung of the earth; "For that which is high to men, is abominable before God."[34]

On the other hand, he would have seen the poor dejected Lazarus to be esteemed and ennobled in the eyes of God and his angels as a precious pearl, which in the end proved true. For Lazarus, as the beloved of God, was carried by the hands

---

[32] Isa. 66:2.
[33] Ps. 112 (113):4, 6.
[34] Lk. 16:15.

The Tenth Step: A Consideration of God's Essence   147

of the angels into Abraham's bosom, and the rich man, as hateful to God, was dragged by the devils into the hell of fire. Now, why do I speak of Lazarus? There is no one higher with God than our Lord Jesus Christ, even according to his humanity, and yet no one in heaven or on earth may be found who is more humble, that would truly say, "Learn of me because I am meek and humble of heart."[35] As much as that most holy soul knows more perfectly than all others the infinite height of divinity, so much the more it knows the lowliness of creation, which was made from nothing, and being itself a creature, it subjected itself to God apart from all others, humbled himself and exalted God, and in turn was exalted by God above all creation, even the angels. We may say the same thing in regard to the blessed angels and the saints. There are none more humble than those who sit higher in heaven, because they who are nearer to God, the more clearly they see how much distance the magnitude of the creator stands apart from the smallness of the creature.

This is why, O my soul, love humility if you desire true glory; imitate the spotless Lamb, imitate his Virgin Mother, imitate the cherubim and seraphim, all of whom the higher they are, the more humble they also are.

Chapter VII
The Throne of the Most High God Signifies Most Blessed Rest

NOT only does God have the highest seat because he judges all, but also because he rests in view of all, and causes them in whom he sits to rest. God's most high throne is his most high rest; for although he governs the whole world in which there are continual conflicts and wars of elements, beasts,

---

[35] Matt. 11:29.

and men, nevertheless he judges with tranquility, as it is said in Wisdom,[36] and he always enjoys the highest peace, nor is there anything which could disturb his leisure and contemplation, in which he has eternal delight. Therefore, he is called the King of Jerusalem, which is the vision of peace. Now, his peculiar throne is upon the blessed angels, therefore it is said: he that sits upon the cherubim.[37] For God is said rather to sit upon the cherubim than upon the seraphim, for the cherubim signify a manifold knowledge, and the seraphim the heat of love; and the rest follow wisdom, but care and anxiety follows love, unless it is accompanied by wisdom. So the soul of a righteous man is also called the seat of wisdom.[38] Moreover, when Isaiah says, "Heaven is my throne,"[39] and when David says, "The heaven of heaven is to our Lord,"[40] by the heaven of heaven is understood the spiritual heavens which dwell upon the corporal heavens, to wit, the blessed angels, as St. Augustine says in his *Exposition of the Psalms*.[41] These heavens God also cause to rest so admirably, that it is a peace which passes all understanding. St. Bernard, in one of his sermons upon the Song of Songs, sets down a very fitting similitude to declare this rest in these words: "God being at rest, puts all things at rest, and to behold his restfulness is to rest. We see a king after daily suits argued before him, to dismiss the company to avoid the troubles of the court and to go at night into his privy chamber with a few whom he loves in familiarity, thinking himself the more sure the more secret he is, and being the more pleasant the more restfully he beholds those few whom he loves."[42] He shows clearly

---

[36] Wis. 12:9, *seqq*.
[37] Ps. 79 (80):2; 98 (99):1.
[38] Prov. 8:12; Isa. 11:2.
[39] Isa. 66:1.
[40] Ps. 113 (114):24.
[41] *Ennarat. In Ps*. CXIII, 2, n. 11.
[42] *In Cant*. Sermo. 23.

enough that God shows himself to the blessed souls, not as a judging master, but as a familiar friend. Now truly, the familiarity which God also shows in this life to pure and chaste minds is incredible. For of him it is said, "My delight is to be with the children of men,"[43] and, "His talk is with the simple."[44]

Hence, all the saints although they suffered pressures in this world, had, notwithstanding, peace in their hearts where God dwelt. Consequently, they appeared and were indeed always joyful and at rest. To them Truth declared, "Your heart shall rejoice, and no man shall take your joy from you."[45]

Chapter VIII
Of the Manifold Depth of the Essence of God

THERE remains the fourth part of the dimension, which is called depth. The depth of God's essence is manifold. First, the divinity is in itself most deep, because it is not superficial and thin, but the fullest and most solid. The Godhead is not like a golden mass that has merely been painted with gold, and has it superficially, but on the inside is brass or wood; rather, like a mass that is wholly golden, vast, and immense, or rather more like a gold mine so deep that no amount of digging will ever empty it. So, God is altogether incomprehensible because, just like a gold mine whose bottom can never be found and which can never emptied by digging, so God whose greatness is without end, can never be so perfectly known by a created mind that it would not always seek to know more and more; and God

---

[43] Prov. 8:31.
[44] Prov. 3:32.
[45] John 16:22.

alone possesses that infinite depth, who alone has the infinite force of understanding.

Next, depth also belongs to God in respect of place, for as he is most high and above all, so he is most deep and under all. Who, as the Apostle says, "Carries all things by the word of his power."[46] So, God, as the foundation and roof of a house, in whom we all "live, move, and are."[47] Hence, Solomon very rightly said, "Heaven and the heaven of heavens cannot contain you."[48] God rather contains the heavens and all things under them, because he is both above the heavens and under the earth.

Furthermore, God's depth is his invisibility. For God is light, but inaccessible; he is truth, but very secret, and interior to every interior: "He has placed darkness as his cover,"[49] David says, and truly he is a "hidden God,"[50] as Isaiah says. St. Augustine, seeking God on one occasion, sent as messengers his eyes from earth to heaven, and all things answered: We are not him whom you seek; but he made us.[51] Therefore, not finding God in the ascent by exterior things, he began to make the journey through interior ones, and truly understood that it is easier to approach God in that way, since he knew that the soul is better than the body, and the internal sense is better than the outward sense, and the understanding, which is still interior, is better than an internal sense. From there he gathered that God, who is more interior than the intellect, is better than the intellect. Consequently, whatsoever we understand or conceive is not God, but some other thing less than God, since God is better than we could possibly conceive.

Well now, my soul, if you are better than the body to

---

[46] Heb. 1:3.
[47] Act. 17:28.
[48] 3 Kg. 8:27.
[49] Ps. 17 (18):12.
[50] Isa. 45:15.
[51] *Conf.* 10, 6.

The Tenth Step: A Consideration of God's Essence 151

which you were given, because it is a body, and you a spirit, and the eye of your body does not see you because it outward, you are inward, so consider that your God is altogether better than you are, because he gives you an intellect, and is like your soul, and therefore, you cannot see because he is a higher and more interior spirit than you are, and in a certain measure, you remain outside, while he is inside in his most secret and deep recess. Will you never be admitted to that secret? God forbid. Your Lord does not lie, when he says, "Blessed are the pure in heart, because they will see God."[52] Nor his apostle, who says, "We see now through the looking glass in darkness, but then face to face."[53] Nor did St. John the Evangelist, lie, when he wrote, "We know that when he shall appear, we shall be like to him, because we shall see him as he is."[54] How great then will you rejoice, when you will see in that secret and sacred sanctuary, and enjoy that light, beauty, and goodness itself! Then it will appear in all clarity how vain, transitory, and of little importance the goods of this earth are: wherewith men, being inebriated, forget the true and everlasting. But if you thirst after the living God, and if your tears are bread unto you day and night while it is said, where is your God?[55] Then do not be slow to cleanse your heart whereby you may see God. Do not tire of arranging the ascensions in your heart, until the God of Gods shall be seen in Sion.[56] Do not grow cold in the love of God and neighbor, nor love by word and tongue, but deed and truth;[57] for that is the way that leads to life.

---

[52] Matt. 5:8.
[53] 1 Cor. 13:12.
[54] 1 Jn. 3:2.
[55] Ps. 41 (42):4.
[56] Ps. 83 (83):8.
[57] 1 Jn. 3:18.

THE ELEVENTH STEP
From the Consideration of the Magnitude of God's Power, by the Similitude of a Corporeal Quantity

CHAPTER I
Of the Breadth of the Power of God.

REAT is the Lord, and there is no measure nor end of his greatness. He is not only great because omnipotence is his height, infinite wisdom his depth, incomprehensible mercy his breadth; and justice like a rod of iron his length, but also for that these attributes are infinite in breadth, length, height, and depth.

Now, that we might begin from his power, or rather, his omnipotence, the power of God finds its breadth, which has been placed in him, in that it extends itself to clearly infinite things. First, it extends itself to everything which has been made. There is nothing in this whole universe of things, from an angel to the lowest worm, and from the highest heaven even to the deepest abyss, which was not made by the power of God, as St. John says, "All things were made by him, and without him nothing was made.... The world was made by him."[1] Secondly, it extends itself to all things that will be made, until the end of days. Just as nothing has been made except by him, likewise, nothing will be made except by him. The Apostle adds, "All things are from him, and through him, and in him."[2] Thirdly, it extends itself to all

---

[1] Jn. 1:3, 10.
[2] Rom. 11:36.

things which can be made, even if they are never going to be. For the angel says, "No word will be impossible with God."[3] And our Lord himself says, "With God all things are possible."[4] Fourthly, it extends itself to the destruction of all things that have been made. Just as God could at once destroy all men and all other living creatures upon the earth by a flood of water, save for a few which it pleased him to preserve within the ark of Noah, so he could use fire to destroy at once not only all men and other creatures found living on the last day, but also all trees, cities, and other things upon the earth. St. Peter the Apostle says, "The day of our Lord will come as a thief, in which the heavens will pass with terrible violence, but the elements will be resolved with heat and the earth and the works which are on it will be burned."[5]

Surely, the breadth of God's power is great, and no man can sufficiently admire it unless he could number all the creatures which God has made, will make or could make. Now, who is able to do this, except he whose knowledge is infinite? This power also may seem the greater, when we imagine how great a thing it is to destroy things made so many ages in one moment, or as Judas Machabeus says, "To destroy with one nod."[6] Let us therefore say with Moses, Who is like unto you among the strong, O Lord?"[7]

---

[3] Lk. 1:37.
[4] Matt. 19:26.
[5] 2 Pet. 3:10.
[6] 2 Macc. 8:18.
[7] Exod. 15:11.

Chapter II
Of the Length of the Power of God

THE LENGTH of God's power is seen by continual cooperation with all the things which he made, and yet neither is, nor ever will be exhausted. It cannot be diminished, weakened, or decayed by any means, since it is joined with true eternity, or rather it is the eternity of true divinity. Many wonder how the sun, moon, and stars can move so long a time with such speed from east to west, and return again to their course without any delay. Surely, it would be worthy of great admiration, except that we know they are carried by God almighty, who carries every word of his power.[8] Others wonder how it can happen that in hell the fire is not consumed which burns forever, nor the bodies of those unhappy men dissolved which are forever scorched in those flames. And this may be thought not only admirable, but also impossible were it not that God, who is all-powerful and eternal, causes that fire to burn in such a way that it is never quenched, and so preserves the bodies of those unhappy men in that fire that they are always tormented and never consumed. Then, others wonder how God carries and endures all things and yet is not exhausted from carrying and enduring so ponderous a burden which is nearly infinite. A strong man, horse, ox, or elephant, can carry a great weight for a time, or a very great weight for a shorter time. Yet, to carry a very great burden for eternity without weariness is beyond the strength of any created thing. Now, others rightly wonder if God would have the power in weight and measure as every created thing has. Now, since the power of God clearly exceeds every measure,

---
[8] Heb. 1:3.

and is itself infinite on every side, it is no wonder if infinite strength can bear a burden no matter how great for an infinite time without tiring out. Let us say then, with the holy prophet Moses, "Who is like to you among the strong, O Lord?"

CHAPTER III
Of the Height of the Power of God

THE HEIGHT of the power of God follows which principally consists in two things.

First, that highness can be called omnipotence because he alone made the highest things. Those which are under the moon, God alone made in the first creation of things, but through the action of creatures they can be generated, transmuted, and corrupted. The elements are in part mutually changed; herbs and plants spring from the earth, beasts are bred of beasts, fish are born in the water, clouds and rain in the air, and comets in the fire. Now, the heavens and the stars, which are the highest bodies, God only created, and he alone preserves in such a way, that no creature has the power to make, change, alter, or corrupt them. "I shall see your heavens, the works of your fingers, the moon and stars which you have founded."[9] For, the Most High kept the highest works for himself only; he began to frame them from their foundation, and has brought them to their perfection. The most high also, by his infinite power, created, preserves, and forever will preserve spiritual things, such as angels and the souls of men, which are the noblest and most sublime works of all, from death. For creatures have no part in making these things; nor can they, all joined

---
[9] Psalm 8:4.

The Eleventh Step: The Magnitude of God's Power 157

together, create or destroy one angel or one soul.

Next, the height of the divine power is very clearly perceived in miracles, which, as St. Augustine teaches, are works beside the usual course and order of nature, whereat the very angels and nature itself marvels.[10] Which of the angels did not marvel to see the sun and moon, which run their course so speedily, stand still at the commandment of Joshua?[11] And that we may not think it happened by some fall, for no man can imagine how a thing so unusual could be done by a mortal man, the Holy Spirit says, "God, obeying the voice of a man."[12] Joshua did not properly speak to the sun and moon, which he knew could not hear his command, but he prayed to God, as if he were to say: By God's command, you O sun, do not move against Gabaon, and you, O moon, against the valley of Ajalon. And the Lord obeyed the voice of a man. Namely, he caused those lights to obey the voice of a man. Often in Scripture the Lord is said to do those things, of which he is the reason that they are done. It is in this way, when in Genesis the Lord says to Abraham, "Now I have known that you fear God."[13] The meaning of those words is: Now I have caused that both yourself and others know that you truly fear God.

Such was also a work signifying the height of divine power, when in the Lord's passion, the moon, which was far away from the sun, approached with incredible speed to the sun and eclipsing it for three hours, caused darkness upon the whole earth, and after with like speed, returned to the place from where it came; all which St. Dionysius the Areopagate, in his epistle to St. Polycarp, witnesses that he saw and observed. This truly is a wonder contrary to the former, though no less strange, for it is as unusual and as

---

[10] *Tract. In Joan.* 24, 1.
[11] Jos. 10:12 *seqq.*
[12] *Ibid.*
[13] Gen. 22:12.

much above the whole power of nature to make the moon run her course faster than normal, as it is to make it stand still. I will pass over the giving sight to the blind, the raising of the dead, and many similar miracles, which God has done and does do by his prophets, Apostles, and his other faithful servants, all which do cry: Who is like to you among the strong, O Lord?

But I cannot omit that chief and greatest miracle, which God will show on the day of judgment, when all the dead will rise together, albeit the bodies of many of them have been burned to ashes and scattered in the winds, or devoured by beasts and changed into other bodies, or buried in fields and orchards and altered into various plants.

Which of the angels will but marvel when they behold in the twinkling of an eye so many millions upon millions of men, at the command of the almighty, to take again their bodies, albeit they have lain hidden for so many ages, and after they have been consumed in so many different ways? Therefore, this is the height of God's power, on account of which it can equally be said, "Who is like to you among the strong, O Lord?"

CHAPTER IV
Of the Depth of the Power of God

THERE remains the depth, which seems to me to be placed in the manner God uses to cause things. Who can grasp the way to make something from nothing? Those men who have stated as a certain and approved principle: *ex nihilo nihil fieri*,[14] could not focus their eyes on this depth. And in this matter, although we believe what we do not see, we believe

---

[14] Nothing is made from nothing.

God who cannot lie. I say, we believe that heaven and earth and all things that are therein were created by God, without any preceding matter from which they were made. Now, how this could be done is a thing too deep for us to discover. Moreover, God did not only make all things from nothing, but also in nothing; namely, without preceding space or a place to contain them in, which is hard to understand, especially in corporeal things. Consequently, this depth is also impenetrable. As St. Augustine says, "Take away the distances of places from bodies, and they will be nowhere and because they will be nowhere, they will not exist."[15] Now, if nothing existed before God created heaven and earth, where did he place heaven and earth? Truly not in nothing; and yet they are created and placed in themselves, because he who can do all things so would and could, although we cannot conceive of how they are done. God himself signified this, when, declaring his omnipotence to Job, said, "Where were you when I laid the foundations of the earth? Tell me, if you understanding, who placed its measure if you know? Or who stretched out the line upon it? Upon what are the foundations of it grounded? Who laid the cornerstone of it?"[16] And that we might understand these works of God's omnipotence, worthy of all praise, the same Lord immediately adds, "When the morning stars praised me together, and all the sons of God shouted joyfully."[17] Namely, the holy angels, which were created together with heaven and earth, and are, as it were, spiritual stars so bright that they may be called the sons of God, when they saw heaven and earth created from nothing and placed in nothing, and yet to be most firmly founded upon their own stability, with wonderful admiration and jubilation they praised the omnipotence of their Creator.

---

[15] *Ep.* 187, 6 n. 18.
[16] Job 38:4-6.
[17] Job 38:7.

It is also no less profound to understand how God, by the only command of his will, erected such vast structures. For we know that in buildings without comparison to lesser ones, how many instruments, engines, and workmen the architects want. So who can conceive how by will alone, which never goes out of the thing that willed, so great and numerous works could be made? God said, though to himself, for the Word of God is in God and is God, I say commanding and expressing the commandment of his will: Let heaven be made: and heaven was made; Let the earth be made: and the earth was made; Let the light be made: and the light was made; Let the sun be made, let the stars, trees, animals, men and angels be made: and they were all made. Add also that the same God can, if he wishes, destroy all things with one nod, as we read in Maccabees.[18] Moreover, it is added to the depth, that God made all of these things which are so many, so great, and composed from so many members or parts in a moment. With us art and nature require a long space of time to perfect their works. We see plants are sown long before they grow; and often many years pass before trees take root, extend their boughs and bring forth fruit. Beasts likewise carry their young ones within them for a long time, and after, they feed them long before they grow large. I will say nothing of art, for experience shows that our artisans can bring nothing to perfection except after a long time.

How great is the power of God, which in a moment brought things that are so great to perfection? I do not mean to make a disputation, however, whether God made heaven and earth and all things in within them in a moment, or whether he spent six whole days in the first creation of things. For I undertake not to clear up questions, but to frame steps to God from the consideration of creation. That

---

[18] Macc. 8:18.

The Eleventh Step: The Magnitude of God's Power 161

which I affirm and admire is that every particular thing was made in a moment by the omnipotent Creator, for of the earth, water, air, and fire there is no doubt, as also of the angels, but that they were created altogether in a moment, of the firmament and division of waters it is also certain that all was done by the powerful word only of the one saying "Let the firmament be made amidst the waters," and indeed in a moment, for it follows, "And so it was done."[19] St. John Chrysostom comments upon this place, saying, "He only spoke, and the work followed." On the words, *Let the earth sprout forth green herbs and so it was done,* he adds: "Who would not marvel to think how at the word of the Lord, the earth should shoot forth different flowers, and adorn her face, as it were, with an admirable embroidery? You might have seen the earth which previously was without form and uncultivated, contend with heaven by its decor and adornment." Later, upon the words, *Let the lights be made,* Chrysostom adds: "He only spoke, and this admirable element was made, namely the sun. What if you add that in the same moment and with the same word the same Creator made the moon and all the stars?" Then on the words, *Let the waters bring forth,* he says, "What tongue can sufficiently praise the Creator? Even as when he said to the earth, let it sprout forth, and presently there appeared great plenty of different herbs and flowers, so here he said, let the water bring forth, and on the spot so many kinds of birds and creeping creatures were made, as no tongue can enumerate."[20]

"Who is like to you among the strong, O Lord?"

---

[19] Gen. 1:11 *seqq.*
[20] St. John Chrysostom, *In Gen. Hom.* IV-VII.

Chapter V
The Soul Is Stirred up to the Fear of God and the Observance of His Commandments

NOW you plainly understand, O my soul, how great the power of your Creator is, whose breadth is infinite, whose length is eternal, surveying and governing all things without growing tired; whose height does things which seem impossible and indeed are, except for him; whose depth makes things in such a way that the manner of it surpasses the understanding of any creature; for he makes them from nothing, and in nothing, without tools and without time, only by his word and command. "He spoke, and they were made; he commanded, and they were created."[21] From where you must gather, if you are wise, how important it is for you to please, and not offend him, and to have him as your friend, and not your enemy, for being offended with you, he can in a moment deprive you of all good, and fill you with all misery; neither is there any that can deliver you from his hands. If being naked and alone you were to meet with your mortal enemy, who assailed you with a sharp sword, what would you do? How would you sweat, look pale, and tremble, and casting yourself on your knees, beg for mercy! And yet, he is a man, so that perhaps you might escape by flight or struggle, or wrest the sword out of his hand, and deliver yourself from death.

Now, what will you do when God is angry, from whom you cannot flee, for he is everywhere, whom you can not resist, for he is all powerful, and whom you cannot delay,

---

[21] Ps. 148:5.

The Eleventh Step: The Magnitude of God's Power 163

since he works in a moment by his sole command. It is not without reason, the Apostle says, "It is horrible to fall into the hands of the living God."[22] Conversely, if you please God, and have him as your friend, who is more happy than you? For he can, if he will, and he will if he is your friend, give you all good and deliver you from all evil. It is also in your power while you live here, to offend and make him your enemy, or to please and make him your friend. For God first by his prophets and after by his Son and his Apostles, does in the Holy Scriptures continually invite sinners to repentance, and the righteous to keep his commandments; that he may thereby have them both to be his friends; or rather his dearly beloved children and heirs of his everlasting kingdom. Hear Ezechiel: "Live I, says the Lord, I will not the death of the impious, but that the impious convert from his way and live. Convert, convert ye from your evil ways: and why will you die, O house of Israel? ... The impiety of the impious shall not hurt him, in whatever day soever he shall convert from his impiety."[23] Then, as Ezechiel speaks, so also does Isaiah, Jeremiah, and the other prophets: for the same spirit spoke alike in them all. Hear the Son of God also, beginning his sermon: "Jesus began to preach and to say, Do penance for the kingdom of heaven is at hand."[24] Listen to the Apostle Paul, speaking of himself and his fellow Apostles in his last Epistle to the Corinthians: "For Christ we are legates, God as it were exhorting by us. For Christ, we beseech you, be reconciled to God."[25] What could be clearer? What more pleasing? The Apostle beseeches us in the name of Christ to be reconciled to God, and to please and not offend him—who can doubt of God's mercy, if he truly returns to him? For he receives them as a

---

[22] Heb. 10:31.
[23] Ezech. 33:11, 12.
[24] Matt. 4:17.
[25] 2 Cor. 5:20.

most loving father receives his prodigal sons which return unto him. And when we are returned and pardoned, what more does he require of us to continue as his children and friends, but to keep his commandments? "If you will enter into life, keep the commandments."[26]

Now, lest perhaps you would say that without God's assistance the commandments cannot be kept, listen to what St. Augustine says of the hardest commandment, namely spending our lives for our brethren: "God would not command us to do it, if he judged it impossible for men to do. If considering your weakness you faint under the commandments, take comfort by the example: for the example concerns you very much. He who gave the example is present also to give you aid."[27] Listen also to St. Leo: "God justly insists upon his command, because he precedes us with his aid."[28]

Why then are you afraid, O my soul, to enter into the way of the commandments, since he runs before you, who by the mighty help of his grace "Makes crooked things straight, and hard roads flat?"[29] By this preceding help, the yoke of the Lord becomes sweet, and the burden light.[30] John the Apostle says, "His commandments are not heavy." But if they seem heavy to you, think how much heavier the torments of hell will be, and do not, unless you are mad, seek to experience them. Think often within yourself, and never forget, that now is the time of mercy, and after of justice; now of freedom to sin, later of intolerable torments for sin; now may a man easily compound with God and with a little labor of repentance obtain a great pardon, and with a short sorrow redeem eternal lamentation.

---

[26] Matt. 19:17.
[27] *Ennarrat. In Ps.* LVI, n. 1.
[28] *De Pass. Dom. Serm.* XVI.
[29] Isa. 40:4.
[30] Matt. 11:30.

The Eleventh Step: The Magnitude of God's Power

Now also, with every good work that proceeds from charity one can obtain the kingdom of heaven; later, not all the wealth of the whole world will obtain one drop of cold water.

THE TWELFTH STEP
From a Consideration of the Magnitude of God's Wisdom Through the Similarity of Corporeal Magnitude

CHAPTER I
The Breadth of the Wisdom of God Lies in the Perfect Knowledge of All Things

HOEVER will attentively consider the breadth, length, height, and depth of God's wisdom may easily understand how truly the Apostle speaks when he says that God alone is wise.[1] Now, to begin from the breadth: God's wisdom is most broad because he distinctly and perfectly knows all things. He does not only know their substances, but also their parts, properties, virtues, accidents, and actions. Hence: "You have numbered my steps,"[2] and "the Lord regards the ways of a man, and considers all his steps."[3] This is why, if he numbers and considers all his steps, how much more will he consider the actions of the mind, whether they are good or bad? And if God "has numbered the hairs of our head," according to his Word, how much more does he know all the members of our bodies, and all the virtues of our minds. If he knows the number of the sands of the sea and drops of rain, we gather from Sirach, how much more may we believe that he knows the number of the stars and angels? Now, if all the idle words of men

---

[1] Rom. 16:27.
[2] Job 14:16.
[3] Prov. 5:21.

were to be judged, as our Lord himself shows, his ears doubtless hear at once all the words of men whether they are corporeal or mental. How infinite, then, is this breadth of wisdom which embraces at once all things that are, have been, will be or might be!

The divine mind does not become more lowly by the knowledge of so many particular lower things, as the foolish wisdom of some philosophers supposed. For perhaps we might think that way if God borrowed his knowledge from things as we do; but since he beholds all things in his own essence, there is no danger of baseness.

Albeit, it is far nobler to borrow knowledge as men do, than altogether to want it, as beasts do; even as it is better to be blind, as sensitive living creatures may be, than without blindness to be unsuited to see, as stones are. Nor are the other members of the body more noble than the eyes, for that they cannot be blind. Now, the eyes are nobler because they can see, although they may also be blind, as St. Augustine truly teaches in the *City of God*.[4] So, my soul, you ought to be careful about what you do, what you say, and what you think in every time and place, since God sees, hears, and marks it. Now, if you dare not do or speak any evil, although goaded by a very pressing desire, if you suppose that you are seen or heard by men, how do you dare to think these things when God sees and is offended? As St. Augustine says, "Suppose no man sees you, yet how will you escape him who looks from above, from whom nothing lies hidden?"[5] And St. Basil, addressing a virgin shut up in her cell, exhorts her to reverence that spouse who is everywhere with the Father and the Holy Spirit, accompanied with countless multitudes of angels and souls of holy fathers: "For there are none among them who do not see all things

---

[4] *De Civ. Dei* 12, 1 n. 3.
[5] *Ep.* 211, 10.

The Twelfth Step: The Magnitude of God's Wisdom 169

everywhere."[6] O happy would you be my soul, if you were always in this company! How perfectly would you lead your life! How diligently would you avoid all fickleness and wandering! For so indeed our Lord said once to Abraham, "Walk before me, and be perfect,"[7] that is, consider that I always see you, and without a doubt you will be perfect.

CHAPTER II
The Length of God's Wisdom Manifests Itself by the Knowledge of Things to Come

THE LENGTH of God's wisdom issues forth in the knowledge of future events. He sees so sharply that he saw from all eternity what will be on the last day, and forever, and no greater length could be devised than this. David says in the psalms, "You have understood my thoughts from afar," and then, "You have known all the last things and them of old,"[8] namely, all things to come and all things past. The books of the prophets are full of the truest and clear predictions, which they did not make themselves, rather, as Zachariah sings, "God spoke by the mouth of his holy prophets, those things which were from the beginning."[9] This prophesying and foreseeing is proper to God alone, as God himself says by Isaiah, "Show what things are to come hereafter and we will know that you are gods."[10] Now, to consider a few things from many, Isaiah speaks in this way, "Thus says the Lord to my anointed Cyrus, whose right hand I have taken, to subdue the gentiles before his face, and to turn the backs

---

[6] *De Virginitate* c. 7.
[7] Gen. 17:1.
[8] Ps. 138 (139):3, 5.
[9] Lk 1:70.
[10] Isa. 41:23.

of kings." In which words the monarchy of the Persians is foretold, and Cyrus, the first king of the Persians, is called by his proper name; the reason is also set down why God would exalt Cyrus, namely to release the captivity of Babylon, all things which were fulfilled about two hundred years later. Daniel likewise, by the similitude of a great statue, "the head of which was gold, the breast silver, the belly and things brass, the feet partly of iron and partly of clay," plainly prophesies the four monarchies of the Babylonians, Persians, Greeks, and Romans; and in the time of the last monarchy, of the kingdom of Christ, namely of the Christian Church, which would be greater than all those kingdoms. Then he describes the wars of the successors of Alexander the Great so clearly that some infidels supposed that they were written after those wars took place. And to pass over the rest, Christ himself, lamenting the destruction of Jerusalem, describes in like manner all things so plainly and with such detail, that he seems to describe the past rather than the future.[11] I skip innumerable other predictions since, as I have said, the books of the prophets are full.

Now, astrologers, and all those who practice divination, who seem to be, as it were, apes of God, must be altogether mocked. It cannot be that they would foretell the truth in regard to future events that are casual or free, unless perhaps they touch upon the truth by accident. Since the will of God presides over and over rules all causes, both necessary, casual, and free, and can — when he pleases — prevent lower causes, none can foretell the truth in anything, except the man whom God will be pleased to manifest his aforesaid will unto, as oftentimes he did unto his prophets. And this is so certain that the devils would be held as gods, principally because they founded oracles and foretold future events, as St. Augustine witnesses in *The City*

---

[11] Lk. 19:41.

The Twelfth Step: The Magnitude of God's Wisdom 171

of God.[12] Now, that excellent doctor of the Church, in his book *On the Divination of Devils*, plainly shows that their divination is as false as their divinity. For they foretell nothing clearly, but what they are planning to do, or, by the swiftness of their nature, relate what has already been done somewhere else, to people who live far away, as if it was a future event, or conjecture that it will take place based on their long experience. In the same way, sailors are also used to foretell many things about the winds, farmers about the rains, and physicians about illness. Now, when the devils are asked about future events which they do not know, they usually answer by ambiguities and equivocation, and when those things prove false, they lay the fault on their interpreter diviners. Consequently, the Lord our God alone, whose wisdom is without number, founds true oracles, and foretells the truth in all things to come, both things that are casual and free.

CHAPTER III
The Height of Divine Wisdom

THE HEIGHT of divine wisdom is the loftiest, and far above the wisdom of men or angels. Height of wisdom is known by the nobility of the object, power, species, and act. The object of the wisdom of God, not only the natural, but also the proportionate, is the divine essence itself, which is so lofty that it is not a proportionate object to the human or angelic intellect. As a result, the highest angels cannot go up to see God unless they are lifted up by the light of glory. This is why God is called "invisible" in the Holy Scriptures, "To the

---

[12] *De Civ. Dei* 2, 24, n. 1.

immortal king of the ages, invisible, the only God."[13] ... "Who alone dwells in the light inaccessible."[14] Power likewise, which is an accident in us, is a divine substance in God, and therefore, higher without comparison than it is in us. The species is also the higher the more it represents, and thereby the angels which have fewer and more universal forms are said to have most knowledge. How great then is the height of the wisdom of God which has no species but his own essence, which being simply one, suffices alone for God to behold himself and all things that have, will or could be made?

Next, that knowledge or wisdom is said to be more noble and also higher, which understands many things by fewer acts. God, however, with one eternal gaze, perfectly knows himself and all other things. This is why the wisdom of God alone is duly considered most noble and high. Now, raise up your eyes, O my soul, and behold how much your knowledge is inferior to the knowledge of your creator. You, discoursing to and fro by many acts, can scarcely know any one thing perfectly, but your creator perfectly and clearly knows himself perfectly by one act, and clearly knows himself and all other things. You, on the other hand, who walks in darkness, may, if you wish, attempt to ascend so high by the wings of faith and charity that, after the laying aside of this mortal body, being transformed from glory unto glory in the light of God, you may see God the light,[15] and being made like unto God, you also with one eternal sight may behold God in himself, and yourself and all other creatures in God. As St. Gregory says in the *Dialogues*, "What does a man not see when he sees the one who sees all things, and how great shall be that pleasure, that glory, that plenty when being admitted to that inaccessible light, you

---

[13] 1 Tim. 1:17.
[14] *Ibid.*, 6:16.
[15] Ps. 35 (36):10; 2 Cor. 3:18.

The Twelfth Step: The Magnitude of God's Wisdom 173

will be a partaker of all the good things of your Lord!"[16] The queen of Sheba, when she had heard about the wisdom of Solomon, and saw the excellent order of the servants of his house, was so astonished that, as Scripture says, "She had no longer spirit, but cried out, Blessed are your men, and blessed are your servants, which stand before you always, and listen to your wisdom."[17]

Now, what comparison is there between the wisdom of Solomon and the wisdom of God, who is the only one that is wise, and wisdom itself? What is the order of his servants in comparison with the nine orders of God's angels, whereof thousands of thousands minister to him, and millions assist him? Surely, if you would even taste a little of these things, would you not move anything, would you not do anything, is there anything you would not gladly suffer to be able to enjoy God? So be humbled, under the mighty hand of God, so that he may exalt you in the time of visitation;[18] subject your understanding to faith, so that you will be raised up to vision; subject your will to obey the commandments, so that you may be raised up to the freedom of the glory of the children of God."[19] Subject your flesh also to patience and labor, so that being glorified, God will exalt it to eternal rest.

Chapter IV
The Depth of the Wisdom of God Principally Lies in the Knowledge of Our Thoughts Which Are to Come

IT REMAINS for us to consider the depth of God's wisdom, which seems chiefly to consist in searching of hearts and

---
[16] *Dial.* 4, 33.
[17] 3 Kings 10:1.
[18] 1 Pet. 5:6.
[19] Rom. 8:21.

reins, namely, in the knowledge of men's thoughts and desires, especially which are to come, which is why we read: "Man sees those things which appear, but the Lord beholds the heart;"[20] ... "You alone have known the hearts of the sons of men;"[21] and, "You have understood my thoughts from afar; my path you have sought out, and you have foreseen all my ways,"[22] and "He knows the secrets of the heart,"[23] and, "The heart of man is perverse and unsearchable. Who shall know it? I the lord, that search the heart and examine its depths."[24] In that place, the Septuagint translates it "How deep and inscrutable is the heart." St. Jerome, explaining this passage informs us that Christ is rightly proven to be God, because he saw the thoughts of men, which God alone is able to see. "And when Jesus, seeing their thoughts; ... But he knew their thoughts; ... Why do you think these things in your hearts?"[25] As a result, every thought and desire of man, although it is present and really exists, is so deep that neither angels, devils nor men can penetrate to that knowledge; but yet a thought or desire in the future is much deeper, since not only are men and angels unable to penetrate it, but also the manner how God, who alone knows it, comes to the knowledge of it.

David seems to have meant to show this in the Psalms, when he says, "Your knowledge has become wonderful of me,"[26] for that "of me" [*ex me*] in the Hebrew phrase means "before me," or "above me". So the sense is: "Your knowledge is more marvelous than I am able to understand." And thus, he adds: "It is made great and I cannot reach it," namely, it is lifted above my knowledge, and I cannot by any

---

[20] 1 Kings 16:7.
[21] 2 Chron. 6:30.
[22] Ps. 138 (139): 3-4.
[23] Ps. 43 (44):22.
[24] Jer. 17:9, 10.
[25] Matt. 9:4; Lk. 6:8; Mk. 2:8.
[26] Ps. 138 (139):6.

The Twelfth Step: The Magnitude of God's Wisdom

means ascend to the understanding of it. He speaks of the knowledge of future thoughts, because he said before, "You have understood my thoughts from afar off, and you have foreseen all my ways,"[27] so he adds regarding the foreknowledge of those thoughts and ways, "Your knowledge is become marvellous of me; it is made great and I cannot reach unto it."

Now, perhaps someone will answer and say that God sees these future thoughts in his eternity, in which all things are present, or in the predetermination of his will; but if that were the case, then wouldn't this knowledge be marvellous? We also know what we intend to do hereafter, or what our present circumstances are. Scripture says that God scrutinizes the depths of the heart, and sees there what a man desires, or thinks, or will desire and think upon later. This is altogether admirable, how God, by scrutinizing the depths of the heart, sees what is not yet there, and what depends upon the freedom of the will, and whether it will come into being some time later. As a result, just as it pertains the height of the power of God, that he would make something from nothing, and call those things which do not exist so that they would begin to exist, so also it pertains to the depth of the wisdom of God, that by scrutinizing the depths of the heart he would see what is not yet there, and if it is not there yet, what will doubtless be there in the future.

CHAPTER V
The Elevation of the Mind to the Divine Physician, Who Searches out and Cures Hearts

SINCE I do not mean to undertake disputed questions but to

---

[27] Ps. 138 (139):3-4.

arouse the soul to be elevated unto God, rouse yourself, O my soul, and lift yourself above yourself, as Jeremiah urges us, and consider that deep abyss of the wisdom of God, which scrutinizes the depth of the heart and sees there many things which the heart itself does not see. O blessed Peter, when you said to the Lord, "Even if I must die with you, I will not deny you,"[28] certainly you did not say that in a two-faced manner, but genuinely, nor did you see the weakness in your heart, which your Lord saw, since he said, "Before the cock crows twice, you will deny me three times,"[29] for your most skillful physician saw the weakness of your heart, which you did not see, and that was true which the physician foretold, and not that which the patient declared. So thank your physician, who as he foresaw and foretold your disease, so by a powerful medicine, divinely inspired penance for your soul, and in short order cured the disease. O good, O pious, O most wise and most powerful physician, "From my secret sins cleanse me!"[30] How many sins do I have for which I have not mourned, nor washed with tears because I do not see them? Give me your grace, with which you search the depths of the heart; and my evil thoughts, desires, and works, which I do not see, you, who see them, show me; and looking back mercifully upon me, produce in me a fountain of tears, that while time serves they may be cleansed and washed away by your grace! Amen.

---

[28] Matt. 26:34-35.
[29] Matt. 26:35; Mk. 14:30.
[30] Ps. 18 (19):13.

THE THIRTEENTH STEP
From the Consideration of God's Practical Wisdom

CHAPTER I
The Breadth of His Practical Wisdom Shines Forth by Reason of the Creation of Things

E HAVE considered the speculative wisdom of God. Let us now consider his practical Wisdom, which we may also call effective. This wisdom has its breadth, length, height and depth. Breadth is understood from creation, the length from the preservation of created things, the height from the work of redemption, the depth from providence and predestination. To begin with creation, God made all things in wisdom, as the Psalmist says,[1] and he has poured it upon all of his works, as Sirach writes.[2] Therefore, just as we recognize the power of the Workman from the creation of all things from nothing, so we admire the wisdom of the Creator in the admirable workmanship which we discern in individual things. He has disposed all things in measure and number and weight, as Wisdom says.[3] Now, God has seasoned all things with this taste, so we may thereby learn to know how savory, amiable, and desirable wisdom itself is. As a result all creation has a certain measure, number, and weight. Firstly, they may be distinguished from God, who has no measure, because he is immense; nor number,

---

[1] Ps. 103 (104):24.
[2] Sirach 1:10.
[3] Wis. 11:21

because he is most perfectly and simply one in essence; nor weight, because his price and value exceeds all estimation. Secondly, that they would be good and beautiful, as Moses truly said, "God saw all things that he had made, and they were exceedingly good."[4]

Thus, all things have that measure which is necessary for them to obtain the end for which they were made, in such a way that there can be no addition or subtraction therein, that the thing would be rendered deformed or useless, and through this rendered less good. "God made all things good in their time; we cannot add anything nor take away from those things which God has made that he may be feared."[5] So God gave the greatest measure to heaven, that it might contain all things below within its embrace; he gave to the air much less than heaven, yet greater than the earth and waters which make one globe contained round about by the air. He gave great measure of body to the elephant, so that he might be able to carry great burdens as well as towers full of men. To the horses he gave a smaller body, because it carries only one rider. He made birds small so that they would hang their nests upon the boughs of trees; he gave bees and ants the smallest of all, so that they would hide themselves in their hives or holes in the earth.

We can say the same thing about number. God only made one sun, because one sun was enough to give light to the whole earth, and with his brightness makes the day. He also made only one moon, which was enough to give light to the night. Nevertheless, he willed there to be a great many stars, so when the sun and moon are absent, as happens during the conjunction of sun and moon, they would in some measure, put away the darkness of the night. He has not only assigned a necessary number to all things in general, but he has also appointed to each thing in particular

---

[4] Gen. 1:31.
[5] Eccl. 3:11, 14.

The Thirteenth Step: God's Practical Wisdom 179

such a number of parts that there can be nothing added or taken away. God has given man two eyes, two ears, two hands, two feet, one nose, one mouth, one chest, one head; and he has appeared a very beautiful and richly honored creature. Now, say this order were to be changed: let a man have one eye, two noses, one ear, to mouths, one hand, one foot, to chests, or two heads, and nothing can be made more unseemly or deformed.

Finally, God has given weight, namely, that estimation to every creature as its nature requires. By the word "weight" or "price" we understand such qualities as make things good and precious; and they are three in number. Necessary parts, that nothing would be superfluous or defective; commensuration, or an apt proportion of parts, and an external amiable color of the body with such internal virtues as shall be profitable and necessary for divers actions. Now, it is marvellous to consider what virtue God has given to certain very small and slender creatures that as his power is in the great, so his wisdom might be seen in small things. Who can conceive what virtue is in a grain of mustard seed, which is the least of all seeds, so that the eye can hardly discern it: and yet, so great a tree lies hidden therein that the birds of the air come and dwell in the branches of it," as the Truth speaks in the Gospel? Nor is it proper to mustard seed only, but common to all other seeds in whose strength lies the roots, stems, branches, leaves, blossoms, and fruit of great trees.

Truly if we did not know this by experience we should not easily persuade men, that from so small a seed so many different and great things could ever spring. Who likewise would imagine that an ant, a gnat, a flea, and such small creatures had feet which speedily move, a head, a heart, inward and outward senses, and prudence and judgment after their manner, although very imperfect? Who also would suppose that in these and suchlike small creatures there should be such force to pierce and enter the quick flesh, that they become not only very troublesome to men, but also to elephants and lions, whom they terrify?

Great, therefore, is our Lord and great is his wisdom, both in great things and in small.

The Prince of Physicians, although an ethnic, did sometimes wonder at the cunning workmanship which God has wrought in a man's hand; and cried out in praise of the Maker.[6] What should you do then, O Christian, who sees that not only the bodies of men and other living creatures, but also the heavens, the stars, the angels, and the immortal souls of men, are made with incredible wisdom by the same most wise Creator?

Chapter II
The Length of the Practical Wisdom of God Shines Forth in the Preservation of Things

MOREOVER, the length of his practical wisdom appears in the preservation of things, as the breadth of it in their creation. This is why the great and admirable wisdom of God is to be observed in the preservation and duration of created things, but especially of such as are corruptible.

First, then, if anyone will but consider how God nourishes and causes grass, plants, beasts, and the bodies of men to grow, and preserves them to the uttermost, he cannot wonder at God's wisdom except with astonishment. He nourishes grass and plants with earth and water, and causes that nourishment to pass from the root to the stock, and from the stock is drawn up by a certain virtue to the boughs, leaves, and fruit, so that it runs into every part after

---
[6] Galen, *de Partibus*.

The Thirteenth Step: God's Practical Wisdom 181

an admirable manner. Men likewise and some beasts he nourishes with herbs, apples, and with the meat of beasts, and causes the nourishment to enter and pass through all parts of the body with such facility and delight as may seem incredible. God deals like a learned and kind physician, who prepares his remedies in such a manner that patients may receive them not only easily, but also willingly. For foods are doubtless medicines, which unless men receive them often they cannot avoid death. Now God, our most loving and skillful physician, has first endowed foods with flavor, so that they may be taken with delight; then he varied them with numberless variety to take away their loathsomeness. And lastly, after different alterations in the mouth, stomach, liver, and heart, he changes the meat into so thin a juice, that it passes without a cut or pain through all the veins and pores of the body unto all the parts of the flesh, bones, and sinews, even when we sleep and do not feel it. The philosophers marvel at the wisdom of nature when they consider these things, but what wisdom can there be in things without life, sense, and reason? So, not the wisdom of nature, but the wisdom of God is to be admired, who made nature and found out the way how these marvellous things might be done. Listen to God's wisdom, speaking in the Gospel: "Consider the lilies of the field, how they grow; they do not labor nor spin, and God clothes them."[7] So, it is not the resourcefulness of nature, but God who causes the lilies to grow, and to be adorned as with clothing. The same thing can be said about the nourishment and growth of all living things, as the Apostle witnesses when he says, "The one who plants is nothing, as well as he that waters, rather it is God who gives the increase."[8] Now, if the wisdom of God feeds, nourishes and preserves animals and vegetation in this mortal life in such a marvelous manner, consider, O my

---

[7] Matt. 6:28-30.
[8] 1 Cor. 3:7.

soul, if you can, how God feeds the minds of men and angels in eternal life. On earth we are fed with earthly foods, albeit they are seasoned with God's wisdom; but in heaven, wisdom itself is the meat and drink of those who live forever. How happy you will be, O my soul, if you could thoroughly penetrate what it is: "God shall be all in all,"[9] what, I say, it is that God, the chief happiness, will be to all the saints food, drink, clothing, life and all things whatsoever. Surely, you would scorn all present things, and only seek and desire those which are above.

Now, let us proceed to the rest. It is likewise similar to a miracle, that in preserving and propagating the life of mortal men, God gave to very weak things a very long and continual motion without a very long weariness. Men altogether labored much to construct a clock in which wheels run by the power of weights for twenty-four hours. How great then is God's wisdom, which causes the nourishing power to work without pause as long as men, beasts, or trees live, and the lungs and arteries move continually seventy years and more. Necessarily, the nourishing faculty must work, and the lungs and arteries must move from the beginning of life until the end. So, men who live until eighty or ninety years must necessarily have their lungs and arteries always move. Now, before the flood, when men lived nine hundred years, their lungs and arteries, which are very delicate and frail, functioned for nine hundred years without pause. Certainly, men who wonder at these things and do not revere and adore God's wisdom in them, necessarily, utterly lack the light of wisdom.

It happens thirdly, that the wisdom of God, although without any labor of men and the other animals or even without the ministry of the sun and other secondary causes, can produce and preserve grass and trees, so that all living

---

[9] 1 Cor. 15:28.

The Thirteenth Step: God's Practical Wisdom 183

creatures might have food at need. Nevertheless, it pleased him to use the service of secondary causes, and the labor and industry of men and beasts, so that nothing would be idle, but everyone might exercise their power.

He also willed that among men, some would be rich and some poor, so that they would all have a chance to love virtue and be tied together in the bond of charity. For the rich may use mercy and generosity, and the poor patience and humility. The rich also need the labor of the poor to till their fields, to feed their cattle, and by different trades provide what is necessary for all. Now the poor need the help of the rich to offer them money and the means to provide food, drink, clothing and other necessities to themselves.

There is also no reason why the poor should complain of God's wisdom. God, who knows all and loves all, has given to everyone what he foresaw to be the most suitable for them to obtain eternal life, just as earthly physicians command some of their patients to be bled, and others to drink wine, eat meat, and engage in recreation. Many poor men, without a doubt, will now be saved who, were they rich, would have perished forever. Now, although the rich may also be saved if they seek to be rich in good works and give willingly of what they have received from our common Lord, not to hide but to bestow, just the same it cannot be denied that poverty is a safer, plainer, and shorter way to heaven than wealth. Our heavenly master does not deceive us when he says, "Amen I say to you, that a rich man shall hardly enter into the kingdom of heaven,"[10] and again, "Blessed are you poor, for yours is the kingdom of God, and woe to you that are rich because you have your consolation."[11] Nor does the Apostle deceive us, when he says, "They that will become rich fall into temptation and

---

[10] Matt. 19:23.
[11] Mk. 6:20, 24.

the snare of the devil and many desires unprofitable and hurtful, which drowns men into destruction and perdition."[12] Yet, what our Lord and his Apostles taught by word, they also confirmed by example: "The foxes have holes, and the birds of the air have nests, but the son of man does not have anywhere to lay his head." The Apostle, speaking of himself and his fellow-Apostles, says, "Until this hour we have hungered and thirsted, and are naked, and are beaten with blows, and are unsettled,"[13] namely they have no place of their own. Nor should we doubt that the wisdom of God's Son and of his disciples chose the safest and clearest way into life. Now, because "there is no end to the number of fools,"[14] i.e. few choose this way willingly, but many turn away from it with all their emotion and strength.

Lastly, the length of God's wisdom is seen in the fact that as it is eternal, so it has endowed all things with a vigorous instinct of self-preservation, as well as to prolong their lives and existence as long as they can. We observe that when men perceive themselves to be in mortal danger, they do as much as they can to save their lives and spare no expense or labor to do so. We also observe animals fight, even above their strength, with those that overpower them, rather than die. We also see a burning candle when it is nearly out, raises itself up two or three times, and sends forth a great flame, as if it were fighting as much as it can not to go out; we observe drops of water hanging sometime upon wood or stone to become round, and to hold themselves together as long as they can lest they fall and perish; we see heavy things go up against nature and light things fall, lest vacuity would happen, and being severed from other things could not be preserved. Now, it is more wonderful that to propagate the species God has endowed

---

[12] 1 Tim. 6:9.
[13] 1 Cor. 4:11.
[14] Eccles. 1:15.

The Thirteenth Step: God's Practical Wisdom 185

parents with so forceful an affection towards their children that it seems altogether unbelievable. We see the hen feed her chickens and fast herself, and though she is weak and feeble, fights most eagerly against birds of prey, dogs and foxes, and what labors and trials women willingly endure to bring their children into the world, and after up in the world, we all know. The reason for this is the counsel of God's wisdom, Who, to maintain this propagation as a shadow of his eternity, has endowed the brutes and the wild beasts, and in all living creatures that have sense, a most vehement love towards their little ones.

There are many kinds of animals and birds which men take great effort to destroy, either for hunting, such as hares, bears, stags, thrushes, quails, partridges, and almost all kinds of fish; or to prevent them from causing harm such as wolves, foxes, snakes, and countless others. As a result, many of those types of animals would have perished long ago if God's wisdom had not, by this love provided for their preservation and propagation. If then, the natural love of all living things for this short and troublesome life is so great, what should our love be toward the blessed and eternal life?

O blindness and folly of man! All things endeavor, even above their strength, to preserve this brief life which is but a shadow of eternity; and man, who has reason, will not strive—I say not above, but only according to his strength—for the eternity of a most happy life. All things by the instinct of nature fear and avoid temporal death above every evil, and man, who is endowed with reason and taught by faith, neither fears nor avoids eternal death as he does temporal evils.

Thus, the preacher spoke true, when he said, "The number of fools is infinite."[15] No less truly is it said in the Gospel, "How narrow is the gate and straight the path that

---

[15] Eccles. 1:15.

leads to life, and few there are that find it."¹⁶

Chapter III
The Height of God's Practical Wisdom Is Seen in the Work of Our Redemption

THE HEIGHT of God's practical wisdom is seen in the work of our Redemption. St. Augustine says, "I was not filled with your admirable sweetness to consider the height of your counsel touching the salvation of mankind."¹⁷ Now surely, it was the highest counsel, by the ignorance of the cross, to repair all the damage which the artifice of the devil has cause by the sin of the first man; and so to repair them, that the work repaired became more beautiful than it was before the reparation.

Four evils were caused by the sin of Adam: injury to God by his pride and disobedience; the punishment of him and all mankind by the loss of God's grace, and of eternal happiness; the sorrow of the angels, whom the injury done to God and the misery fallen to man did very much displease; the triumph of the devil and all the wicked spirits, who rejoiced to see man overcome and cast down by them. All of these evils the wisdom of God removed by the mystery of the cross, and turned them to greater good, so that not without cause does the church sing: *O felix culpa*, namely, "O happy fault, which merited so great a Redeemer!" Certainly, if a new and valuable garment were torn or ripped in some accident, a mender by his skill and a new adornment added so restores it, that it becomes more elegant and precious, it would rightly be said O happy

---

¹⁶ Matt. 7:14.
¹⁷ Confess. 9, 6 n. 14.

tearing, which gave the occasion for such a favor. The first man, however, by the cunning and envy of the devil was puffed up in pride, and pretended a similitude of God, and disobeying God transgressed his precept; so in a certain measure he pillaged the honor due to God. Now Christ, the second Adam, who is the wisdom of God, "humbled himself, being obedient even to death,"[18] and restored so much greater honor to God than that which the first Adam stole away by his pride and disobedience. Adam was a pure man, and if he had obeyed God he would have obeyed in a very easy matter. Why was it such a difficult thing for the first humans to abstain from the fruit of the forbidden tree, when the fruit of many and more excellent trees abounded? As a result, their sin was the greater, in proportion to how much easier their obedience, since it required no labor. Christ, on the other hand, was true God and man, and he humbled himself to obey God his Father in a thing that was very hard and laborious, namely, in the death of the Cross, which was full of pain and ignominy. Hence, if we consider the excellence of the person as well as the depth of his humility and obedience, nothing can be thought greater, or more meritorious and showing honor to God than that humble obedience of Christ.

As a result, our Lord spoke most truly in the Gospel when he said, "I have glorified you on earth,"[19] since Jesus Christ did glorify God his Father with unspeakable glory before the angels of heaven and before all the souls of the prophets and others, to whom these things were known. Now, if the angels at Christ's birth, for the humility of the crib, sang, "Glory to God on high,"[20] with much greater joy did they sing it for the humility of the cross.

Moreover, had man not sinned, he would have obtained

---

[18] Phil. 2:8.
[19] Jn. 17:4.
[20] Lk. 2:14.

the supreme equality of the angels; now, however, through the redemption which is in Christ Jesus, the human race has obtained that one man has been exalted above all the angels to sit at the right hand of God, and is the head and master of angels and men. For so the Apostle Peter writes about Christ, "Being gone into heaven, angels and powers and virtues being made subject to him," and his fellow Apostle Paul says, "For that very thing God also has exalted him, and given him a name which is above every other name, that in the name of Jesus every knee shall bow, in heaven, on earth and under the earth."[21] So in an indescribable manner, the Son glorified the Father in the humility of the passion, and the Father glorified the Son in the exaltation to his right hand, likewise in an indescribable manner. Such a glorification overflows so wonderfully to the whole human race, that truly they are the most ungrateful who do not acknowledge such an infinite benefit, and fail to thank God for it. Why? Not only Christ, God and man, but his mother is exalted above all the choirs of angels, though she is not God, but a human creature. This is why men, since they have received more glory than they would have had if the first man had not sinned, may justly cry out, "O happy fault which has merited such a redeemer!"

Hence the holy angels became sorrowful for the fall of the first man, as for the grievous calamity of their younger brother, so likewise they became glad through the copious redemption accomplished through Christ. For if there is joy in heaven before the angels over one sinner that does penance,[22] how much greater may we believe was the joy before those angels, when they say God's justice fully satisfied by Christ, a man for mankind, and by the key of the Cross the kingdom of heaven opened to all believers? Nor should we suspect that the angels took it badly because God

---

[21] Phil. 2:9-10.
[22] Lk. 15:7.

The Thirteenth Step: God's Practical Wisdom

raised up Christ and the Blessed Virgin with greater excellence than those angels; the angels lack all spite and envy, and are full of the truest, most burning charity. Charity is not envious, nor is not puffed up; it is not sorrowful for another's good, but rejoices with all the righteous for their happiness no less than for her own. The Church, therefore, truly sings, "Mary has been assumed into heaven, the angels rejoice." It does not say that they are sorrowful, rather they rejoice to see the Virgin Mother of God exalted above the choirs of angels to the heavenly kingdom. The angels also know that God has done it most justly, Who does all things in perfect wisdom and justice, and their will is so united to God's will by the insuperable bond of love, that whatever pleases God pleases them likewise, and can not displease them in any way.

The devil however, although he triumphed for a time because he had overcome and cast down the first man, nevertheless became more sorrowful after. The victory of Christ brought it about that now, not only men as Adam was, but also women and children assault and gain triumph over the devil. It would have been no disgrace for the devil to have been overcome by Adam in paradise, when he had no ignorance or weakness, but was armed with original justice, which did in such sort subordinate his sensual part to reason that it could not rebel, until his mind first rebelled against God. On the other hand, for the devil to be overcome now by a mortal man that is a pilgrim, and subject to ignorance and concupiscence, is a terrible disgrace. Yet, he is so overcome by the grace of Christ that many have triumphed in chastity, patience, humility and charity, although he does not cease daily to cast his fiery darts of temptation and persecution. Herein, the height of God's wisdom is so much to be admired. God foresaw that the contempt of temporal riches, of fleshly pleasures, and worldly honors, which are the snares of the devil and drown men into destruction and perdition,[23] was necessary for mankind against the deceits of the devil. What then did he devise that would cause these things to become bitter to men, and the contraries, i.e. chastity, poverty, humility, patience, and contempt of the world to become sweeter? He came down from heaven, and having received the form of a servant, rendered that necessary but bitter medicine into a sweet and attractive remedy by his example. So much so, that many men now love fasting more than feasting, poverty more than riches, virginity than wedlock, martyrdom than self-indulgence, to obey than to command, and to be humbled than to be exalted. Who, seeing God in the form of man, to be poor, humble, patient, continent, and, what is more wonderful, fastened to a Cross, and willingly shedding his precious blood from burning charity, will not be inspired and rouse to imitate him?

This was the wonderful invention of the high and marvelous wisdom of God, of which Isaiah sings: "Make his inventions known among the people."[24] Nevertheless, this high wisdom of God seems like foolishness not only to the wise of this world, as the Apostle says,[25] but even to carnal and sensual men who believe in Christ, but refuse to follow in the footprints of Christ; the Apostle calls these men the enemies of the cross of Christ.[26] Now you, my soul, endeavor to take in the honey from the rock, and oil from the hardest stone, i.e., the wisdom from foolishness, the wisdom of God from the foolishness of the cross. Attentively and diligently discover who it is that hangs upon the cross, and why he hangs there. Then, when you will have discovered that he is the one "who sits above the Cherubim,"[27] nay more, "who

---

[23] 1 Tim. 6:9.
[24] Isa. 12:4.
[25] 1 Cor. 2:14.
[26] Phil. 3:18.
[27] Ps. 98 (99):1.

The Thirteenth Step: God's Practical Wisdom 191

sits on the right hand of Majesty on high,"[28] you will easily understand that he does not hang on the cross for his crimes, nor due to his weakness, nor by the power of others, but willingly on account of the burning desire to make satisfaction to divine justice for the sins of the whole world, and for the honor and glory of God the father, for the eternal salvation of all the elect, as the Apostle says, "That he might present to himself a glorious church, not having spot or wrinkle."[29] Lastly, for your sake, because he loved you and delivered himself for you, "a sacrifice and oblation to God unto the odor of sweetness."[30] When, as I say, you will find these things to be true, love such a benefactor from the bottom of your heart, seek to follow him, and begin to thirst ardently after the glory of God, and the salvation of all nations, but especially after the beauty and glory of the whole Church and your own eternal salvation. Begin to hate iniquity with all of your soul, and thirst after purity of heart and perfect justice, so that at length, you might also desire to be a partaker of your Lord's cross in tribulation and affliction, that ever after you would rise with the just to glory and not with the wicked to punishment.

Chapter IV
The Depth of the Practical Wisdom of God Consists in His Providence and Predestination

THERE remains the depth of practical wisdom, which consists in the providence and predestination, as well as the judgments of God. For it is written, "Your judgments are a

---

[28] Heb. 1:3.
[29] Eph. V:27.
[30] Eph. 5:2.

great deep."[31] Now first, the providence of God is altogether admirable, because he immediately governs all created things, and directs them to their ends. As the wise man says, "He has equal care of all,"[32] namely, God has care of all things without exception, so that a little sparrow will not fall upon the ground without God's providence, as our Savior says.[33] A man that can number the multiplicity of things of the whole universe may in some sort be considered as partaking of the wisdom of God, the sole ruler and governor of every thing, and every individual thing. One supreme Pontiff can indeed rule the whole Christian world with general providence, but not particular, which extends itself to each individual Christian; therefore, he calls many bishops to take part of that care. Now, one king may govern many provinces by general providence, but not by particular, which concerns every subject, and as a result, he has many viceroys, deputies, and supervisors. God, on the other hand, has as much care of every one in particular as of all in general, and of all in general as every one in particular. "God does not forget a little sparrow,"[34] "the hairs of our head are all numbered by him,"[35] and not one of them will perish, since his watchful providence is always upon us. Young ravens that have been forsaken by their parents are not forsaken by God.

O my soul, how safely may you rest in the bosom of such a Father, although you were in darkness, among the mouths of lions and dragons, among innumerable legions of innumerable spirits. Cling to God with a true love, a holy fear, a hope that does not fail, and a faith that does not doubt.

---

[31] Ps. 35 (36):7.
[32] Wis. 6:8.
[33] Lk. 12:6; Matt. 10:29.
[34] Lk. 12:6.
[35] Matt. 10:30.

The Thirteenth Step: God's Practical Wisdom 193

Now, God's providence does not only take care of present and particular things, but also "reaches from end to end, powerfully, and disposes all things sweetly."[36] This is why God is called the king of ages,[37] for he has established the order of the ages, and disposed the succession of kingdoms, and the changes and variety of seasons from all eternity. To God, nothing can happen that is strange, unlooked for, or unthought of; "But the thoughts of mortal men are fearful, and our providences uncertain."[38] For we have nothing but spurious conjectures about future events, whereas God knows all things to come as certainly as things past and present, and disposed in his mind before the making of the world the order and succession of all things. As a result, our holy mother the Church publicly and securely affirms that God's providence does not err in the order and disposition of things. Now, because the reason of God's providence is most secret, and his judgments are great a great deep, it happens that some men, seeing many evils are committed among men and left unpunished, they fall in to that ruin, that they believe human affairs are not governed by God's providence, or that those evils are committed by God's will. Both of these opinions are wicked, but the second is more evil, as St. Augustine writes.[39] They run head long into these errors, who see part of divine providence, but not all of it. Whereas they should expect the end of things, which will be made manifest to all on the day of Judgment, they rashly judge before the time and are greatly deceived. As a result, the Apostle cries out, "Judge not before the time, until our Lord comes, who will lighten the hidden things of darkness, and will manifest the counsel

---

[36] Wis. 8:1, and the antiphon *O Sapientia*, for Vespers on 17 Dec.
[37] 1 Tim. 1:17.
[38] Wis. 9:14.
[39] *De Ord.* 1.

of hearts."[40] St. Augustine declares this with an excellent similitude. "If a man were to behold in a checkered pavement the workmanship only of one small piece of it, he might blame the workman as ignorant of order and composition, namely, because he only sees one portion of the work, but not the greater part. Now, if he saw all the parts and how they come together, he would, without a doubt, very much commend both the work and the workman."[41] Thus, many men see the impious live prosperously, and the just conversely oppressed and afflicted; they do not know what God preserves for the future, either for the iniquity of the wicked, or the patience of the just, and thus they break out into blasphemies with those who said to Job, "God walks about the poles of heaven, and does not consider our affairs,"[42] and with others, which say in Malachi: "Everyone who does evil is good in the sight of the Lord, and such please him. Where is the God of judgment?"[43] St. Augustine uses another similitude taken from poetry. If anyone begins to hear an epic poem, and will say in the beginning or in the middle of it that it is not good, he will be justly rebuked for his foolishness; for he should wait until all the syllables were sounded, and then he might find fault with it if he did not like it. So they are altogether very foolish who dare to rebuke the providence of God before the whole order of providence has run its course.

So, O my soul, if you are wise, endeavor all you can not to do evil, for thus God commands you. As to why he permits evil to be done, leave it to his judgments, which may be secret, but cannot be unjust.

---

[40] 1 Cor. 4:5.
[41] *Ibid.*, n. 2.
[42] Job 22:14.
[43] Malach. 2:17.

The Thirteenth Step: God's Practical Wisdom

CHAPTER V
On the Depth of the Mystery of Predestination and Reprobation

NOW, although the notion of God's providence in the governance of human affairs is a great abyss, just the same, the notion of eternal predestination and reprobation is an abyss deeper without any comparison. Why would God fill many wicked men with temporal goods and leave their sins unpunished in this life, and conversely, why does he permit many innocent men to be pressed by need, unjustly troubled, beaten, and even killed? We cannot investigate each particular thing, but we can assign some general cause with a degree of probability. God often makes the wicked abound in temporal goods, to reward some of their good moral works, albeit he will not give them eternal life; or to allure them to be converted from their sins by that fact, and to be brought to the hope and desire of eternal benefits. Sometimes, he also does not punish their sins in this life because he will sufficiently punish them in hell. The just, on the other hand, he permits to be afflicted with poverty, ignominy, and other various afflictions, to purge their venial sins in this life, as also to reward their patience, humility, and other virtues with greater glory in eternal life. Now, who can say why God loved Jacob and hated Esau before they did either good or evil? This is what the Apostle marvels at in his Epistle to the Romans. They were twins, brothers born of the same father and mother, and yet God by predestination loved the one and by reprobation hated the other.[44] Lest perhaps, some might say that God foresaw the good works of the one and the evil works of the other, the Apostle prevents the answer, saying, "This was done that

---
[44] Mal. 1:2-3.

the purpose of God according to election might stand."⁴⁵ And he brings forth the words of God to Moses, "I will have mercy on whom I have mercy, and I will show mercy to whom I will show mercy."⁴⁶ Who will not likewise wonder that one should persevere a long time in good works, as Judas the traitor, and at the end of his life give over and perish: and another to continue a long time in evil works, as the good thief, and at the end of his life be converted and go into Paradise? Now, you will say, Judas betrayed Christ, and the thief confessed Christ. It is true, but could not Christ have looked on Judas as he looked on Peter, and inspired Judas with that powerful grace which no hard heart can refuse? And could not Christ have given faith and repentance to both of the thieves who were crucified with him, as he did to one of them? Could he not suffer them both to die in their sins, as he suffered one of them? Who likewise can say why God takes away some, lest malice would change their understanding,⁴⁷ and yet does not take away many, but permits them to fall from virtue to vice, and to end their days in it? What shall we say of whole nations, some of which may be called to faith very soon, others after a long time, without which none can be saved? "For he that does not believe has already been judged."⁴⁸ As the Apostle says, "Everyone who shall call upon the name of the Lord shall be saved. How then shall they call upon him whom they have not believed? Or how will they believe him whom they have not heard? And how will they hear without a preacher? How shall they preach unless they are sent?"⁴⁹

These are the highest and deepest secrets, which the eternal Father has hidden in the depth of his wisdom, which

---

⁴⁵ Rom. 9:11.
⁴⁶ Exod. 33:19.
⁴⁷ Wis. 4:10.
⁴⁸ Jn. 3:18.
⁴⁹ Rom. 10:13-15.

the Apostle does not open, rather marvels when he says, "O depth of the riches of the wisdom and knowledge of God! How incomprehensible are his judgments, and his ways unsearchable! For who has known the mind of the Lord? Or who has been his counselor?"[50] This alone is lawful for us to know, that in God there is no wickedness, and that at the last day there will only be those who will truly say: you are just, O Lord, and your judgments right."[51] Furthermore, this secret is advantageous for us all. Thereby it comes to pass that the wicked will not despair of their salvation, nor the righteous presume upon it. Good men will also not lose hope for the conversion of the wicked, rather, they will pray for all, and carefully seek their salvation. And again, none, no matter how good and holy they may be, will have occasion to be proud, rather, work out their salvation with fear and trembling.[52] Now you, O my soul, since you have considered all of these things, labor in earnest that you will do good works by your calling and election, as Peter warns.[53] What those good works are, which make sure your calling and election, St. John teaches when he says, "My little children, let us not love in word or in tongue, but in deed and truth."[54] For charity is a virtue with which none shall be damned, and without which none shall be saved. It is shown by the works, namely when one gives alms to the poor, or forgives his enemies, for the true love of God and his neighbor, and not for hope of temporal reward, or for inordinate love of creatures.

Now, since it is not enough to begin well, "He that will persevere to the end, shall be saved,"[55] consequently, the Apostle says, "work", i.e. attentively, carefully, and

---

[50] Rom. 11:33-34.
[51] Ps. 118 (119):137.
[52] Phil. 2:12.
[53] 2 Pet. 1:10.
[54] 1 Jn. 3:18.
[55] Matt. 10:22; 24:13.

diligently follow the business of your eternal salvation. Truly, there is no sign more probable of God's election than when a man, being more careful of his salvation than of any other thing, prays continually to God for the gift of true repentance, true humility, perfect charity, and perseverance unto the end; and not being content with prayer alone, he also endeavors to seek and find with all of his strength the kingdom of heaven and its justice, as our Savior exhorts us.

THE FOURTEENTH STEP
From the Consideration of God's Mercy

CHAPTER I
The Breadth of God's Mercy, Whereby He Removes Our Miseries

N THE SCRIPTURE, the Holy Spirit elevates the mercy of God with wondrous praises, to the extent that he does not hesitate to proclaim it above all the works of God. So David sings: "Our Lord is sweet to all, and his mercies are over all of his works."[1] We will easily examine the greatness of this divine attribute if we take a moment to consider attentively the breadth, length, height, and depth of it.

The breadth of God's mercy is seen in the fact that he alone can take away all miseries, and from all created things he takes away some for the love he bears them, and not for any benefit to himself. Created things can certainly take away some miseries, as bread takes away hunger, and drink thirst, clothing nakedness, knowledge ignorance, and so in regard to the rest. No created thing, however can abolish every misery. Furthermore, there are some miseries the greater they are, the more secret and inward they are, and God alone can apply the remedy to them. Such are the subtle snares of the demons, who are many, mighty, and have wicked designs against us. Such are the errors of our mind and conscience, which we ourselves do not see in us; we often appear to ourselves to be inwardly in the best of

---

[1] Ps. 144 (145):9.

health, when we labor gravely and very dangerously. Who can deliver us from these miseries, but our all powerful physician alone? Now, he also often mercifully delivers us from them without our knowledge, for which reason we may all justly be called unkind to God, as our Lord himself witnesses when he says, "That his heavenly Father is kind to the ungrateful and the evil."[2] For we scarcely know the least part of God's benefits, and therefore we thank him not for them with such devotion and humility as we should.

Created things cannot take away all miseries, but only a few; they do not even abolish them from all men, but from a few. God alone can take away all miseries from all, and albeit he does not do so, nevertheless there is no man who is not a partaker of some of God's mercy. Thus the prophet rightly sings, "The earth is full of the mercy of the Lord."[3] The Church also says in her official prayer at Requiem Masses, "O God, to whom it is proper to have mercy, etc." This is because it pertains to him to remove misery, who lacks misery, and all miseries pertain to him alone to remove all miseries from all, who alone altogether lacks every misery. Moreover, who altogether lacks misery except for God alone, who is pure act, and the supreme good, and whose essence is beatitude? O my soul, if you could conceive what the life of your Lord and father is, which is exalted above all misery and is happiness itself, how would you sigh from your heart to be in the his bosom, that of you also it might be said, "Evil will not approach you, and no plague will approach your tent!"[4] But you will say, if God can take away all miseries from all things, why does he not do it, since he is the "Father of mercies,"[5] namely, a most merciful Father? Why are there so many miseries in

---

[2] Lk. 6:35.
[3] Ps. 32:5.
[4] Ps. 90 (91):10.
[5] 2. Cor. 1:3.

mankind under the government of the Father of mercies? Why is it also said, "The earth is full of the mercy of the Lord,"[6] and not rather more vice versa: The earth is full of all misery? God truly can take away all miseries, yet he alone takes away those which his wisdom judges fit to be taken away. But his wisdom judges that it is not expedient for men that all should be taken away; for it is mercy sometimes not to take away some misery so that a place might be prepared to for even greater mercy.

The Apostle prayed three times to our Lord that the prick of the flesh might be taken from him, and he was not heard, because power is perfected in weakness.[7] God did not take from Lazarus the misery of poverty and sores, so that with greater mercy he might be carried by the angels into Abraham's bosom.[8] Now, how should the rich exercise the works of mercy if no one was poor, hungry, thirsty, naked, sick, pilgrims, and imprisoned? If there were no temptations nor combats with demons, where would be the triumphs and crowns of virgins and confessors? If there were also no labors and sorrows, where would be the crown of patience? If there were no persecutors, where would be the crown of martyrs? Now, it is true that in this exile the earth is full of miseries, for sins alone are great miseries; and it is also true that the earth is full of mercy of the Lord because the conversion of sinners, the merits of saints, and other almost infinite benefits of God, both spiritual and temporal are nothing other than the great and continual mercies of God our creator. Let us give thanks to our good Lord, because just as our tribulations abound in this pilgrimage, so also our consolation abounds by his mercy. "O Lord, your mercy is in heaven," David says. For there shall be mercy without misery, because mercy will altogether remove all misery.

---

[6] Ps. 32:5.
[7] 2 Cor 12:7, 9.
[8] Lk. 16:19 *seqq.*

Chapter II
The Length of the Mercy of God Is His Longanimity or Patience

THE LENGTH of his mercy is longanimity, or patience, which Scriptures usually joins with mercy as a part, or rather a species of it. David speaks in this way: "The Lord is compassionate, long-suffering, and plentiful in mercy."[9] Truly the longanimity and patience of God, our most merciful Father, toward the human race is altogether admirable, and we do not find the like either in masters towards their servants, or parents towards their children, albeit they are both men. First, God is long-suffering toward sinners, waiting for them with incredible patience, sometimes from their first childhood to their last old age, permitting them to blaspheme his name and to break his law, and meanwhile "being beneficial to them from heaven, giving rains and fruitful seasons, filling their hearts with food and gladness."[10] Now, what master or parent is there among men who is so merciful and gentle, who seeing himself injured and scorned for a long time by his servant or child, would not at long last put them out of his house? Yet the mercy of God is not overcome by man's malice rather, "He acts patiently, not willing that any perish, but that they all return to penance."[11] The wise man says, "You have mercy on all, O Lord, and you ignore the sins of men for the sake of repentance."[12]

Furthermore, this patience seems greater still in that many sinners, since they are brought out of the lake of misery and from the mud of the rotting dregs by God's

---

[9] Ps. 102 (103):8; 144 (145):8.
[10] Acts 14:16.
[11] 2 Pet. 3:9.
[12] Wis. 11:24.

grace. Being called from the penalty of eternal death to the adoption of the sons of God and the hope of the heavenly kingdom, again and again, often and more often to the old foulness and ingratitude. Nevertheless, they are not forsaken by the longanimity of God, rather, they are most lovingly awaited and invited to repentance; and if they truly repent, as prodigal sons, they are received by their most merciful Father to the kiss of peace and to their former dignities.[13] It is not without reason that the Lord answered St. Peter, who asked how often he should forgive a brother as often as he sins against him, or only until the seventh time, saying, "I do not say to you until seven times, but until seventy times seven."[14] Evidently, what he does in offering forgiveness to sinners is the same thing he wills us to do. Moreover, he placed no limit to reconciliation, except the end of this life; however long the sinner lives, even if it's a hundred years or more, and though he arrives by falling and falling again, he is admitted by the most merciful Father with forgiveness of his sins. No penance is too late for the mercy of God, provided it is in earnest, and from a truly contrite and humbled heart. As a result, no one should abuse the mercy of God, and delay his conversion from day to day, when no man knows in what hour or on what day he is going to depart his body, and be subject to the tribunal of the most just Judge. Nay more, all should be encouraged and enticed to conversion by this very incredible goodness of God. Now, if the Lord is so merciful to sinners who so often relapse, how great will be the sweetness of the Father toward us, who, after we have once tasted the grace of God, can never again be induced to be separated and estranged from it by the force temptations?

Now, there is another longanimity of God wonderful and loveable beyond measure, which he uses to put up with the

---

[13] Lk. 15:11, *seqq.*
[14] Matt. 18:21-22.

offenses of the just. For God caused us, by his boundless mercy, to become his friends when we were his enemies, his sons when we were servants, and heirs of his kingdom when we were guilty of eternal death; and still, our ingratitude is such, that daily we render him evil for good. If James says, "In many things we all offend,"[15] what ought we say, who stand at so long a passage of time from the perfection of the apostles? Lo, we speak in prayer with God, and straight away we are torn away by the imagination to other thoughts, as though we have turned our back on God. What master in this world would allow his servants to stand in his presence, and speak with him, and at the spur of a moment to turn away, neglecting him, and gossiping with the servants? What might I say about idle words? Vain thoughts? Fruitless labors? Excess in food, drink, sleep and play? Neglect of holy things? Failure to give fraternal correction? What might I say about any other of the numberless offenses whereby we have all continually offended? And yet our God, "sweet and mild, full of mercy to those who call upon him,"[16] puts up with this rudeness, incivility (that I might speak in this way), and trifling of his sons, which certainly men would not tolerate from other men. St. Augustine remarks about this in his treatise on Psalm 85, commenting on these words: "O Lord, you are sweet and mild," where he laments human weakness in avoiding the distractions of the mind during times of prayer, and magnifies the mercy of God in putting up with so many injuries of his servants.[17] For he knows our frame, and acts with us in the same way as a mother with her infant, whom she cherishes and nourishes although perhaps it might strike her. Now, although God permits so many of our offences without breaking the bond of friendship, or depriving us of

---

[15] Jas. 3:2.
[16] Ps. 85 (86):5.
[17] *Ennar. In Ps.* LXXXV, n. 7.

The Fourteenth Step: God's Mercy

the right of our inheritance, nevertheless, he will not forgive them unavenged on the day of judgment, when we shall render an account for idle words, unless he will find them already cleansed by tears, prayer, or another kind of satisfaction. Now, lest perhaps you, my soul, might consider these trivial offenses, and therefore, with this self deception would neglect them, listen to what St. Bonaventure says about St. Francis, a man truly illuminated by the divine light: "Greatly did he think he offended, if being at his prayers his mind wandered after vain figments of the imagination. Whenever such a thing happened, he did not delay confession, but made satisfaction on the spot. He so turned this zeal into a habit, that he was very rarely disturbed by a fly of this kind. Once, during Lent he made a little basket to pass away some short period of time without being altogether unoccupied; but while he was saying Terce the memory came into his mind for a short time and distracted him. Being so moved by the fervor of spirit, he burned the basket, saying: 'I will sacrifice it to the Lord, whose sacrifice it impeded.'"[18] Thus, distraction of mind in time of prayer and praising God is no small offense as many imagine; but great is the mercy and longanimity of God our Father, in that he is not grievously angered, nor does he immediately punish us on that account.

---

[18] *Vita S. Franc.* 10, 7-8.

Chapter III
The Height of the Mercy of God is Known from the Cause Moving It

NEXT follows the height of God's mercy, which is taken from the cause moving God to mercy. Now truly it is most high, and exalted above all the heavens according to the Psalmist, "Lord, your mercy is in heaven," and, "Mercy will be built up forever in the heavens."[19] Some men have mercy upon other men because they need their help; and this is the lowest degree of mercy, since it does not go beyond one's own advantage. In the same way we have compassion for our horses, dogs and cattle. Others have mercy because of kinship or friendship, namely because they are sons, or brothers, or acquaintances or friends, and this degree is a little higher, and begins to have the notion of virtue. At length, others have mercy because they are neighbors, i.e. men as they are, created by the same God and from the same earth; hence they do not distinguish whether they are friends or enemies, good or bad, countrymen or foreigners, rather they have mercy on all whom they know to have been created in the image of God; and this is the last degree to which mortals can ascend. God, however, has mercy on all things because they are his creations, and he is especially merciful to mankind, because they are his images; and still he is more merciful on the just, because they are his sons, heirs of the kingdom, and coheirs of his only begotten Son. But if you were to ask, why God created the world, why he made man to his image, why he justified the wicked and adopted them as his sons, constituting them heirs of his kingdom, then altogether no response could be made except that he willed. And why did he will it? Only because he is good, for goodness pours itself out, and gladly shares itself.

---

[19] Ps. 35 (36):6; 88 (89):3.

Thus, mercy is built up in heaven,[20] and from the highest habitation, from the heart of the supreme Father, it descended to earth, and filled it, as the Prophet sings: "The earth is full of the mercy of the Lord."[21] Consequently, God found in himself the reason to have mercy on us; he found in us the reason to punish us. Now, my soul, raise the eyes of your mind to that fountain of mercy on high, look to that supreme purity, not mixed with an intention of its own convenience. And when you hear the master of all exhorting and saying, "Be merciful, as also your Father is merciful,"[22] strive with all of your might not only to have compassion for your fellow servants, but to have it with that pure disposition with which the heavenly Father has mercy on you. If you forgive the injury caused by your detractors, forgive from he heart, handing all offense to perpetual forgetfulness, for even our Father forgets our sins, as Ezechiel writes,[23] and as far away as the east is from the west, he makes our iniquities from us,[24] so that they may not be able to harm us further. If you give alms to the poor, know that you receive more that you give; because the man who has mercy on the poor lends to the Lord.[25] So give humbly and reverently, not as alms to the poor, but as a favor to the Prince. If you suffer any inconvenience to benefit your poor neighbor, think yet how far you come short of your Lord, who to benefit you gave his blood and life. So will you, without hope of earthly reward, and without any motion of vainglory, merely for the love of God and your neighbor, profit in the virtue of mercy.

---

[20] Ps. 88:2.
[21] Ps. 32:5.
[22] Lk. 6:36.
[23] Ez. 28:22, 24.
[24] Ps. 102 (103):12.
[25] Prov. 19:17.

Chapter IV
The Depth of God's Mercy Is Seen in its Effects

IT REMAINS to consider the depth of God's mercy. As the height of it appears chiefly in the cause, so the depth of it is seen particularly in the effect. That mercy which is limited to words is not said to be deep, but rather shallow and superficial; that which comforts the needy not just with words, but also deeds is deeper; that which not only comforts them with words and deeds, but also endures labors and sorrows for their sake, the deepest. Now our God, whose mercy is without number, has been merciful to us in all of these ways. First he sent us letters to comfort us, namely the Holy Scriptures, as Maccabees says, "We have for our comfort the holy books which are in our hands."[26] He does not speak to us by letters alone, but also by the words of preachers, which are legates of Christ for our reconciliation,[27] and by interior inspirations promising us his assistance and protection. "I will hear what the Lord God shall speak in me, because he will speak peace upon his people, and upon his saints and upon them that are converted to the heart."[28]

Secondly, the benefits of the mercies of God against our manifold miseries, both spiritual and temporal, are so many that they cannot be numbered. For everywhere "he crowns us in mercy and compassion,"[29] namely, he surrounds us on all sides with the benefits of his mercy.

Thirdly, God's mercy descends by the mystery of the holy Incarnation to labors and sorrows, to hunger and thirst,

---

[26] 1 Macc. 12:9.
[27] 2 Cor. 5:19-20.
[28] Ps. 102(103):4.
[29] Ps. 102(103):4.

to ignominy and reproaches, to stripes and wounds, and to the death of the cross to redeem us from our sins, and from eternal death due unto us for it. Is there any greater depth to which God's mercy could descend? Certainly. He did all these things not from a debt, but a favor. "He was offered because he willed."[30] For who compelled the Son of God, who, who did not think it a robbery to be equal with the Father, rather he emptied himself, taking the form of a servant.[31] To be made poor for us, that by his poverty we might become rich.[32] To be humbled unto death, even death on the cross to exalt us.[33] Truly love alone compelled him, mercy alone constrained him. It also descended even further, since he would bestow upon us honor and glory in the work of our salvation. That division which the angels made seemed fitting enough: "Glory to God in the highest, and peace on earth,"[34] honor to good, and profit to men. Yet, God's mercy would have all the profit to be ours, and part of the glory to be his and part of it to be ours. For he would give us his grace, whereby we might work out our salvation. Not that the merit of Christ was insufficient, but to communicate with us the praise and glory of our own salvation. Not that the merit of Christ was insufficient, but to share with us the praise and glory of our own salvation. This is why it is said in the Gospel, "Pay them their wage."[35] And the Apostle boasts, saying, "There is laid up for me a crown of justice."[36] Lastly, God's mercy is the deepest toward men, especially toward the just and them that fear God, because it exceeds the affection of fathers and mothers, which is the greatest we can find on earth. Listen to Isaiah:

---

[30] Isa. 53:7.
[31] Phil. 2:7.
[32] 2 Cor. 8:9.
[33] Phil. 2:8.
[34] Lk. 2:14.
[35] Matt. 20:8.
[36] 2 Tim. 4:8.

"Can a woman forget her child, that she will not have pity on the son of her womb? And if she would forget, yet I will not forget you."[37]

Then David: "As a father has compassion for his children, so the Lord has compassion on his children, so the Lord has compassion on them that fear him."[38] And lest you might say there are some parents whose love sometime changes into hatred, David adds more about God's mercy and love toward his children. "The mercy of our Lord from everlasting upon them that fear him,"[39] the duration of which the Apostle renders secure when he called God the Father of mercies, and God of all consolation.[40] So God is not only a Father to those that fear him, but a most merciful Father ever ready to comfort us: for he takes away such miseries and afflictions from his children as he judges expedient to be taken from them, and therein he shows himself to be the Father of mercies; and he gives them unspeakable comfort to suffer those which he judges to be inexpedient for them to be taken away, and thereby he shows himself to be the God of al consolation. Yet the Apostle says "of all consolation" for two reasons.

First, because God comforts those that are his in all kinds of tribulation, which truly the world cannot do, for oftentimes it understands not the causes of tribulations, even as Job's friends were "heavy comforters" as he called them, because they did not know the cause of his grief, and therefore applied the remedy where they should not,[41] or else the tribulation is sometimes so great that no earthly consolation can equal it. Yet God the all powerful and most skillful physician, can cure every infirmity and therefore, the

---

[37] Isa. 49:15.
[38] Ps. 102 (103):13.
[39] Ps. 102 (103):17.
[40] 2 Cor. 1:3.
[41] Job. 16:2 *seqq.*

The Fourteenth Step: God's Mercy

Apostle says, "who comforts us in all our tribulations."[42] Then he is called the God of all consolation, because he comforts so fully that it would be better to suffer tribulations with such a comforter than to want them both together. Such a thing happened to a young man called Theodorus, a confessor in the persecution of Julian the Apostate, who being tortured ten hours together with such cruelty and change of executioners as in no age is reported the like, sung notwithstanding all that while with great joy the Psalms of David, and when it was commanded he should be let down, he began to be sorrowful, because of the great comfort he received by the presence of an angel while he was being tortured, as Rufinus writes.[43] This is why it is no marvel if the Apostle says, "I am filled with consolation, I do exceedingly abound in joy in all our tribulation,"[44] and "Who comforts us in all our tribulation, that we also may be able to comfort them that are in all distress."[45]

What does it seem to you, my soul, of this very ample, continual, pure and infinite mercy of our Lord, who needs nothing of ours, and yet out of the abundance of his love is so careful of his servants, as though all his happiness depended on them? What thanks will you give him now? What can you ever do, not to be ungrateful to such great mercy? Seek at least all you can to please him. Now, because it is written, "Be ye merciful as also your Father is merciful,"[46] and "Have mercy on your own soul, pleasing God."[47] Begin first diligently to find out the miseries of your soul, since the miseries of the body are as plain as day; so that it is needless to put a man in mind of them: for if the body is one day without food and drink, or one or one night

---

[42] 2 Cor. 1:4.
[43] *Hist. Eccles.* 10, 36.
[44] 2 Cor. 8:4.
[45] 2 Cor. 1:4.
[46] Lk. 6:36.
[47] Eccl. 30:24.

without sleep, or be hurt by a fall or wound, it cries out and complains, and is looked into with great care. But the soul fasts whole weeks from her food, and is sick with wounds, or perhaps dead, and no one takes care or has compassion for her. Visit your soul often, examine all of her powers, whether they are well and profit in the knowledge and love of true happiness, or whether they are sick with ignorance or languish with divers desires. Also whether the mind is blinded with malice, or the will infected with envy and pride. And if you find any such thing, cry to our Lord, "Have mercy upon me, because I am weak."[48] Seek spiritual physicians and apply fit remedies. Take compassion likewise of other souls, whereof an infinite number perish, although Christ died for them. O my soul, if you truly knew the price of souls, namely the precious blood of the Son of God, and also the great slaughter which is made of them by the infernal wolves and roaring lions, the devils; surely you could not but from your heart take pity on them, and by your prayers to God, and by all other means seek to deliver them.

Lastly, also take compassion on the corporal necessities of your neighbors, "not in word and tongue only, but in deed and truth;"[49] having in mind the saying of our Lord: "Blessed are the merciful for they will obtain mercy."[50]

---

[48] Ps. 6:3.
[49] 1 Jn. 3:18.
[50] Matt. 5:7.

THE FIFTEENTH STEP
From the Consideration of the Greatness of God's Justice, by the Similitude of a Corporal Quantity

CHAPTER I
The Breadth of God's Justice is Universal Justice

OD'S justice in Holy Scripture is received in four ways: first for universal justice in general, which contains all virtues and is the same with sanctity or probity. Thus in the Psalms: "The Lord is just in all his ways and holy in all his works."[1] Secondly, for truth or fidelity, so in another psalm: "That you would be justified in your words."[2] Thirdly for distributive justice of rewards. "There is laid up for me a crown of justice, which the Lord will render to me on that day, a just judge."[3] Fourthly and lastly, justice avenging sins. So in another psalm, "He will rain snares upon sinners, fire and brimstone and blast of storms, the portion of their cup, because the Lord is just and has loved justice."[4]

The greatness of God's justice will appear to us if we consider the breadth of it in general; the length of it, namely his truth and fidelity, the height of his justice, namely distributing rewards in heaven, and the depth of it, punishing the wicked eternally in hell.

Now we will begin from the breadth. This is called

---

[1] Ps. 144 (145):17.
[2] Ps. 50 (51):6.
[3] 2 Tim. 4:8.
[4] Ps. 10:7, 8.

justice in general among men, which disposes a man to behave himself well in all actions according to all laws. And in that all virtues, both theological and moral are included. There is also another virtue which contains all virtues in her bosom, and commands and directs all acts of virtue to the last end, which is called charity. Such a virtue, although it is particular in itself, and one of the theological virtues, nevertheless it is also rightly called universal justice. For it disposes a man to be good to God and neighbor, and through this it embraces all things. The Apostle says, "Charity works no evil ... He that has charity fulfills the Law ... Charity is the fulness of the law."[5] St. Augustine also says, "Inchoate charity is inchoate justice, charity increased is justice increased; great charity is great justice, perfect charity is perfect justice."[6]

Moreover, all the virtues are in God, which supposes no imperfection, and in place of those things which presuppose imperfection, there is something by far better and more excellent: and through this no goodness is lacking to it; rather his goodness and holiness is infinite, so that he has earned the best cause to be called the only good and the only holy one.[7] Faith is not in God a theological virtue, because faith is "of things which are not seen,"[8] whereas God sees all things. Nor is there hope in God, because hope is the expectation of things to come; but God awaits nothing, for he possesses all things from eternity. Nor is there in God repentance for sin, because God cannot sin. Nor humility, for humility keeps a man from rising vainly above himself, and to persevere in his state; God has nothing above himself to which he may seek to ascend, because he is the most high. Yet charity, the queen of virtues, is in God most fully

---

[5] Rom. 13:8, 10.
[6] *On Nature and Grace*, 70, n. 84.
[7] Heb. 11:1.
[8] Matt. 19:7.

The Fifteenth Step: The Greatness of God's Justice

and truly infinite. He loves himself with an infinite love, because only he perfectly knows the infinite good, which is his essence; likewise, he loves all the things which he made. Thus Wisdom speaks: "You love all things which are, and hate none of the things which you have made."[9] God knows to separate good from evil by his wisdom, namely, the defect from nature, even in demons and the most wicked men, and he loves nature which he has made, and hates the defect which he did not make. Moreover, there is such true charity in God, that he would be called charity, as St. John says when he writes, "God is charity."[10] Our love, being compared with God's love, is very small, for there are many things we do not love, because we do not know them, since we do not discern good in them from evil. Many good things also we do not love well, and therefore, not with true charity, because we are wicked and serve lust rather than love. We love God with an imperfect charity, not only because we do not love as much as his goodness merits (and not even the angels have obtained such a measure), but also because we love less than we ought, and even less than we could if we were to labor more vigilantly and diligently in prayer and meditation. This queen of virtues in the Lord of virtues is accompanied with singular magnificence, extravagant generosity, incredible kindness, unheard of patience and longanimity, more than paternal piety and sweetness, never failing truth and fidelity, mercy filling heaven and earth, a most right and inflexible justice, lastly, the purest and brightest sanctity, so that in his sight the stars of heaven are not clean. The stupefied seraphim shout: Holy, Holy, Holy Lord God of hosts."[11] O my soul, if you considered these matters attentively, with what fear and trembling would you serve God in your prayers and devotion! Especially at the

---

[9] Wis. 11:25.
[10] 1 Jn. 4:16.
[11] Isa. 6:3.

holy altar, with what reverence and humility would you offer up to the eternal Father his only begotten Son in the sight of angels, for the health of the living and the dead!

CHAPTER II
The Length of God's Justice Is Discovered by Its Truth and Fidelity

NOW, let us continue. The length of God's justice is manifested by its truth and fidelity. The promises of God, which were declared many ages ago by the prophets, never were nor shall be in vain, rather, they are firm and stable, even more so than heaven and earth. Thus says our Lord: "It is easier for heaven and earth to pass away than one speck of the law to fall."[12] And our Lord means by the law, not only the truth of his commandments, but also of all the promises, for whatever he has commanded must be observed, or punishment will follow, and what he promised has been made firm by eternal strength. This is why the Lord also says, "Heaven and earth will pass away, but my words will not pass away,"[13] and Isaiah: "The word of our Lord remains forever,"[14] and David, "All of his commands are faithful, confirmed for ever and ever."[15] Lastly, the Apostle says, "But God is true and every man a liar,"[16] "It is impossible for God to lie."[17] The reason for these sayings is, because being Wisdom he cannot be deceived, being Goodness, he cannot deceive, and being Omnipotence he

---

[12] Lk. 16:17.
[13] Matt. 24:35.
[14] Isa. 40:8.
[15] Ps. 110 (111):8.
[16] Rom. 3:4.
[17] Heb. 6:18.

cannot fail. Men, although they may be wise, good, and strong, may be deceived and deceive, because they neither know all things nor can they perform all things as they will. Men who are good when they make a promise may shortly thereafter become evil and not fulfil their promise. As a result, if you are wise, my soul, trust in God alone; adhere to him alone, and cast all of your cares upon him. Walk carefully with your Lord God, and he will be careful of you. Be as careful as you can lest you might offend his justice, and his mercy will always so defend you, that you will not need to know what man or demon can do to you.

Chapter III
The Height of God's Justice is Seen in the Bestowal of the Heavenly Reward

THE HEIGHT of God's justice is discerned in the payment of heavenly reward, which God himself, as the supreme and most just Judge, has prepared for those who lived piously and justly. First, we shall discern the greatness of his justice if we compare God as a judge with men who are judges; then if we compare the rewards with rewards, namely, the rewards which God will give with those which men usually give.

Men who are judges, whether princes or prelates, also have under them subjects or servants, for the most part do not give just rewards to those that serve them, and for many reasons. Either they cannot, through want of ability, give all according to their deserts; or they know not all of their deserts, or they know not their true worth which depends upon the sincerity and affection of their minds; or through covetousness and malice, or some other perverse inclination, they will not justly reward their just labors; or lastly, they are either prevented by death before they can pay the recompense which they owe; or those to whom it is due die before they begin to taste the fruits of their labors. Nevertheless, God gives the just not only the rewards they deserve for their good works, but also above what they deserve. What merit can be produced more vile and obscure than to give a cup of cold water to one that is thirsty? Yet, for it also God has promised a reward.[18] Of the large rewards which our Lord has promised, St. Luke writes: "Good measure and pressed down, and shaken together and running over, shall they give into your bosom."[19] There is no danger that God would fail in anything to reward the righteous, since he is the Lord of all things, and by his word alone, could increase and multiply them without end. Nor should there be any doubt, lest perhaps he be deceived in the true number and value of what they have merited, since he is most wise and beholds all things, searching the hearts and bowls of his well-deserving servants to see with what mind, intuition, zeal, and diligence they do all things. Nor may it be thought that God has an ill meaning to defraud his children and servants of their due rewards, because he is faithful in all of his words. Lastly, he cannot die, because he is more immortal than anything whatsoever; in this way there is no danger that death would prevent them from receiving what is due to them. Therefore, it is the safest thing to do business with God in the notion of labor and reward, and most perilous and foolish to place trust in men, and also expect just rewards for their labors.

Now, let us compare rewards with rewards, heavenly things and divine, with terrestrial and human things. What, I ask, can men render to those who labor all day, watch all night, and hazard their lives for them in battle? O blindness of men! What can they render but small, cheap, and abject

---

[18] Matt. 10:42.
[19] Lk. 6:38.

The Fifteenth Step: The Greatness of God's Justice   219

things, which will continue but a short period? God renders great, high, and eternal things; yet are the other desired and these scorned. St. John Chrysostom[20] compares the palaces, cities, and kingdoms of this world, which men so admire, to houses of clay which children make with great labor. Verily, these little huts and small buildings are made by the children with great labor, nevertheless they were clearly mocked by their elders, and often even when a father or a teacher sees little children occupy themselves with trifles while they omit their studies, he will take his foot and destroy them all, so it happens that what they had made with great time and labor, he more easily overturned in a moment. In this way, great palaces, towers, arches, cities, and the kingdoms of mortals, are mud huts if they are compared with the heavenly and eternal goods, and they are mocked by the blessed Angels looking down from heaven, and often are overturned by our heavenly Father so that we might understand how clearly empty they are. Albeit now only a few notice this, nevertheless, on the day of Judgment everyone will see, although that sight will be of little help to them. St. Hilary says, "The day of judgment will reveal how all of these things were vain."[21]

Now, let us explain a little more precisely what these heavenly rewards are, which many now scorn in favor of a little earthly recompense. First, in the kingdom of heaven there will be most, or rather all good things that can be desired: everyone who lives there will be happy, and happiness is defined to be an accumulation of all good things perfectly gathered together. So the goods of the mind will be there, namely beauty, health, and strength, and external goods, such as wealth, delight and glory. Furthermore, all of these things will be in a most high, perfect and excellent degree. God, who showed his power in creating the world

---

[20] *Hom.* 24 *in Matt.*
[21] *Comment. In Matt.* 10, n. 16.

from nothing, his wisdom in the rule and providence of it, his charity and goodness in the redemption of the human race by the mystery of the Incarnation and Passion of his Son, will then show the splendor of his glory and bountifulness of his generosity in rewarding with palms and crowns those which have triumphed over their enemy the devil. There wisdom will not be the speculation of divinity in created things, but the very clear vision of the essence of God, the cause of all causes, and of the very first and supreme truth, whereby that most beautiful the souls of the saints will shine by a light so splendid, that St. John, speaking about that future glory, says, "We will be like unto him, because we will see him as he is."[22] From the highest wisdom charity will proceed, the queen of virtues and so fervent that they will always adhere to God in such a way that they cannot and will not be separated from him. In this way the whole soul, and all its power will remain constituted in the best state, and the body will shine as the sun, as our Lord himself witnesses when he says, "Then the just will shine as the sun in the kingdom of their Father."[23] This shall be the beauty of it; health, will be the immortality and strength impassibility. Lastly, that which is now a natural body will then be a spiritual body,[24] i.e. so obedient to the spirit, that it will exceed the winds in agility and penetrate the walls through subtlety.

Hence, there will be riches, both because they will be in need of nothing, and because with God and in God they will possess all things. "I will place them over all his goods."[25] What shall I say of their delight, since it is written: "They will be drunk with the plenty of your house, and with the

---

[22] 1 Jn. 3:2.
[23] Matt. 13:43.
[24] 1 Cor. 15:44.
[25] Matt. 24:47.

The Fifteenth Step: The Greatness of God's Justice 221

torrent of your pleasure you will make them drink."[26] What mind can conceive how great a delight it is to enjoy the supreme good? To see beauty itself? To taste sweetness itself? To enter into the joy of our Lord, namely, to become partakers of that delight which makes God happy? The honor and glory of saints exceeds all eloquence. Amidst the theater of the whole world, of all men and angels, the saints will be praised by God, and crowned as champions, and placed on Christ's throne as partners of his kingdom, which is the greatest honor of all. For so we read in the Apocalypse, "He that shall overcome, I will give him to sit with me on my throne, as I also have overcome, and have sat with my Father on his throne."[27] At this height of honor, the prophet marveled when he said: "To me your friends, O God, have become most honorable, their principality is exceedingly strengthened."[28]

Now, if we were to add to this multitude and excellence of goods the ineffable seasoning, eternity, who can imagine the greatness of this heavenly happiness? Yet, what we cannot now imagine in thought, we will prove in deed, if by living piously, justly, and soberly, we will finally arrive in that happy country. For those goods will continue forever, which now with momentary labors the servants of Christ purchase by means of his grace. What do you say, O my soul, to these things? Are you pleased to imitate the games of children in building little houses from clay and being deprived of the possession of a truly eternal kingdom? Are you pleased (which the mind shudders to think) to take pleasure in the delights of beasts, when you are invited to the ineffable joys with the Angels? O Lord, may your mercy turn this away from the soul of your servant. Rather, pierce

---

[26] Ps. 35 (36):9.
[27] Apoc. 3:21.
[28] Ps. 138 (139):17.

my flesh with your fear,[29] and let the obedience of your law be sweeter to me than honey or the honeycomb,[30] so that crucifying my flesh with the vices and concupiscences of it, I may aspire to the spiritual and eternal pleasures of your paradise. Grant to your servant, O Lord, to follow the steps of your Christ, who meek and humble of heart, "when he was reviled did not revile, when he suffered he did not threaten."[31] Grant that I may live soberly, justly, and piously in this age, so that with some confidence I may expect the blessed hope, and arrival of the glory of our great God and Savior Jesus Christ.

Chapter IV
Of the Depth of God's Justice, Whereby He Prepared Everlasting Punishment for Sinners

IT REMAINS that we consider the justice which God will use in punishing sinners in the uttermost depths of hell. This is why if we mark with attention and diligence we shall certainly understand that what the Apostle teaches is very true, when he says, "It is horrible to fall into the hands of the living God."[32] Now, to follow the method we observed regarding justice rewarding the merits of the saints, God the just judge will punish all sins though never so small, as, for example, an idle word, for we read in the Gospel: "Every idle word that men will speak, they will render an account for it on the day of Judgment."[33] Men leave many offences unpunished, either because the offenders resist or flee, or

---

[29] Ps. 118 (119):120.
[30] Ps. 19:11.
[31] 1 Pet. 2:23.
[32] Heb. 10:31.
[33] Matt. 12:36.

The Fifteenth Step: The Greatness of God's Justice 223

because they do not know whether they are done or not, or perhaps the matter is not sufficiently proven by witnesses, or else they will not punish them, being either bribed, oppressed with favors, or depraved by their own malice. God, however, is all powerful, so no one can resist his power; he is everywhere, so nothing an be hidden from his sight. "Where will I go from your Spirit, and where will I flee from your face? If I will ascend into heaven, you are there, if I descend into hell, you are there."[34] He is the wisest, and knows everything, even those things hidden in the deepest depths of the heart. Nor does he need witnesses to prove offenses, since men's consciences will be against them as a thousand witnesses. Finally, neither bribes nor favors can corrupt his justice, since he does not need our goods. So, it is certain that there is no sin, whether it is the greatest, or the least, moral or venial, which can escape the avenging justice of God unless it is first purged by repentance. The more copious his mercy is in forgiving in this life, his justice will be more rigid and severe in avenging after this life. The Prophet Isaiah speaks about this life when he says, "In the acceptable time I have heard you and on the day of salvation I will help you."[35] The Apostle explains this when he says, "Behold, now is the acceptable time, now is the day of salvation."[36] In regard to the time after this life, however, the prophet Zephaniah cries out, "That day, a day of wrath, a day of tribulation and distress, a day of calamity and misery, a day of darkness and mist, a day of cloud and whirlwind, a day of the trumpet and sound."[37]

Sins will not only be punished, but punished with dreadful punishments which will be so remarkable that scarcely any living men would venture to conceive of it. Just

---

[34] Ps. 138 (139):7-8.
[35] Isa. 49:8.
[36] 2 Cor. 6:2.
[37] Zeph. 1:15-16.

as eye has not seen, ear has not heard, and it has not entered into the heart of man what God prepared for those who love him, so altogether eye has not seen, nor ear heard, nor as it entered into the hearts of men what God has prepared for those who hate him. The punishments for sinners in hell will be many, the most terrible and pure, i.e., not mixed with any comforts, and eternal, which infinitely increases their misery. I say that they will be many, because every power of the soul and every sense of the body will have their own torturers. Carefully assess the words of the sentence of the supreme Judge related in the Gospel: "Depart from me you cursed, in to the eternal fire."[38] He says, "depart from me" namely, go away from the company of the blessed, deprived of eternity in the vision of God, which is the highest and essential happiness, and the final end for which you were made. "Cursed," i.e. do not hope any longer for any kind of blessing, you will be deprived of all the luster of grace, of every hope of salvation. The water of wisdom will no longer rain upon you, or the dew of good inspiration, the ray of heavenly light will no longer shine, the grace of repentance will not sprout in you, nor the flower of charity, the fruit of good works; the Dawn from on high will not visit you now and forever. Nor shall you only lose spiritual and eternal goods, but also corporal and temporal; you will have no riches, no delights, no comforts, but you will be like the fig tree which, when I cursed it,[39] the whole thing immediately withered to the root. "Into the fire," namely, into the furnace of burning and inextinguishable fire,[40] which will not only take in one member, but all the members together, and strike them with the most excruciating punishment. "Eternal," i.e. in the fire which does not need the kindling of wood to burn always, but is kindled by the mere breath of

---

[38] Matt. 25:41.
[39] Matt. 21:19.
[40] Matt. 13:42.

The Fifteenth Step: The Greatness of God's Justice 225

God almighty. This is why Isaiah rightly cries out, "Who will be able to dwell with the devouring fire?" "Who will dwell with everlasting flame?"[41] No man will be able to bear it patiently, but impatiently and with indignation, and they will be compelled to bear it with despair, even if they do not wish to. And he adds: "Their worm will not die, and their fire will not be extinguished,"[42] and our Lord repeats this more than once in St. Mark.[43] The worm of conscience is added, and of the memory of this time, wherein the wicked could, if they had wished, have escaped those punishments with little effort and enjoy eternal joy. Now, lest someone would suppose that the damned receive some comfort by walking or moving from place to place, listen to what our Lord himself says, "Bind his hands and feet, and cast him into outer darkness, where there will be weeping and gnashing of teeth."[44] Therefore, those unhappy men, bound hand and foot with eternal bonds, will always lie in the same place without the light of the sun, moon or stars, burning in flames of fire, weeping, tormenting, and gnashing their teeth through insanity and despair. Nor will those who have been thrust into the fullest place of dread merely suffer the most terrible pains in hell, but also extreme poverty of all things, and disgrace, ignominy as well as confusion. In an instant they will suffer the loss of palaces, fields, vineyards, cattle, beasts, clothing, and lastly, gold, silver and precious stones. They will be brought to such wretchedness, that with the rich reveler he will desire a drop of cold water; he will long, and wait, and will not be heard. Furthermore, these proud and boastful men, who in this life would not suffer any injury, and put their dignity before all things, will see all of their crimes revealed in the theater of the whole human

---

[41] Isa. 33:14.
[42] Isa. 56:24.
[43] Mk. 9:43, 45, 47.
[44] Matt. 22:13.

race, and all the angels, even though they were carried out in darkness or hidden in security of the heart, although they were the foulest crimes, treason, thefts, incest, and sacrileges. As the Apostle says that when our Lord will come to judge the world, he will illuminate those things hidden in darkness, and he will manifest the intentions of hearts, and then every man of God will have praise,[45] and certainly every wicked man will receive rebuke from God. Yet, the disgrace and confusion of the wicked in that theater will be so great that St. Basil did not hesitate to say that it will be the greatest of all punishments,[46] especially for hypocrites and the proud and boastful, who were honored as a god or rather as an idol in this world.

Now, if what we have said of the loss of all goods both heavenly and earthly, not to mention the most painful sufferings, and the ignominies and disgraces were going to have some end, or at least be mixed with some type of consolation or relief, just as the miseries of this life, they might in some manner be considered tolerable; but since it is absolutely certain that as the happiness of the blessed will continue forever without any mix of misery, so likewise, will the unhappiness of the damned will continue forever without any mix of comfort. So truly, they are blind and stupid who do not labor with all of their strength through whatever tribulations and dangers, infamy and death, which the Apostle calls momentary and trifling,[47] to obtain the kingdom of heaven and heavenly beatitude.

---

[45] 1 Cor. 4:5.
[46] *In Ps.* XXXIII.
[47] 2 Cor. 4:17.

CHAPTER V
Why the Punishment of the Damned Will be Everlasting

IF ANYONE were perhaps surprised that God, who is most merciful, has appointed such severe and continual punishments for the sins of men, which are pass very quickly and do not even seem that serious, let him listen to St. Augustine: "Whoever thinks this condemnation is too rigorous or unjust, he does not know how to measure truly the wickedness of sin where there is such ease in not sinning; ... who can sufficiently declare how wicked a thing it is not to obey in a matter so easy, commanded by so great a power, and threatened with such great punishment?"[48] St. Augustine speaks of Adam's sin, but the reasoning is the same regarding all sins. If we set up scales with true weights, and not false ones, we will find that every mortal sin is very grave and from three headings.

For, it is a horrible thing for the creature not to obey the Creator, since the dignity of the Creator is infinitely distant from the lowliness of the creature. The creature is also the servant by nature, and by nature the Creator is lord, and whatever the creature has, it received from the Creator; but the Creator receives nothing from it.

Next, if the commands of the Creator are burdensome, nevertheless the creature should obey them; but "his commandments are not heavy,"[49] and our Savior says that his yoke is sweet and burden light. Consequently, how baffling is it for the little worms of the earth not to obey their Creator in such an easy matter? Besides, if God had not

---

[48] *City of God*, 14, 15.
[49] 1 Jn. 5:3.

threatened the punishment of eternal death to sinners, men would, perhaps, have excused their sins. Yet, seeing that he has so often and so clearly threatened it by his prophets and Apostles, what sinner can excuse his contumacy?

Lastly, if the sin of damned men were not eternal, we might wonder why the punishment of it should be eternal; but seeing that the obstinacy of the damned is eternal, why would we wonder if their punishment is also eternal? And this obstinate will in evil, which is common to the damned and in the demons, this perverse will, I say, turning them away from God, the highest good, which remains immovable and stable, causes holy men to fear a mortal sin more than hell fire.

Listen to what Eadmerus, an Englishman, writes about St. Anselm: "My conscience bears me witness, I do not lie, that we have often heard him [Anselm] protest by the testimony of truth, that if he would corporally behold on the one hand the horror of sin, and on the other the pains of hell, and that of necessity he must be drowned in one of them, he would rather choose hell than sin."[50] Another thing he used to say, which may seem as strange to some as the former, namely, that he would rather have hell without sin than the kingdom of heaven with sin. If this holy man did speak and feel these things, being illuminated by God, he knew that sin was more grievous than the pains of hell; how much more will God, who penetrates the malice, uncleanness, and perverseness of sin to the bottom, truly judge that the punishment which he has appointed from all eternity is most due to them?

O my soul! Do not be deceived, nor seduced. Do not become like those "Who say they know God, but deny him with their deeds."[51] Many men have faith by habit, but not by act, like a sword in a scabbard. If they did actually

---
[50] *Vita*, l. 2.
[51] Tit. 1:16.

The Fifteenth Step: The Greatness of God's Justice

believe, and while believing, seriously consider that God is faithful and just, and has indeed prepared dreadful and everlasting punishments, without any comfort for the wicked, it could not be that they would do the things which they do, and drink, as it is said in Job, "iniquity as water,"[52] namely, so easily, so cheerfully, and so without fear commit many great sins, as if rewards and not punishments were due to sinners. You, I say, believe most firmly and in belief consider that God is in this life a Father of mercies, and ready to pardon mercifully the sins of all who truly repent, and that after this life he will become the God of vengeance, and execute the punishments he has prepared for them, and by his prophets and Apostles commanded to be preached, and committed to writing for the memory of posterity.

In this way it will come to pass, that by fear of intolerable punishments, and the hope of the greatest rewards, as though they were lifted up on two wings, you will pass the perils of the present life in safety, and obtain rest and everlasting life. Amen, Amen.

FINIS

---

[52] Job 15:16.

FINIS

www.ingramcontent.com/pod-product-compliance
Lightning Source LLC
Chambersburg PA
CBHW011405070526
44577CB00004B/404